Instagram®

by Jenn Herman, Corey Walker, and Eric Butow

for
dümmies®
A Wiley Brand

Instagram® For Dummies®

Published by: **John Wiley & Sons, Inc.**, 111 River Street, Hoboken, NJ 07030-5774, www.wiley.com

Copyright © 2023 by John Wiley & Sons, Inc., Hoboken, New Jersey

Published simultaneously in Canada

For general information on our other products and services, please contact our Customer Care Department within the U.S. at 877-762-2974, outside the U.S. at 317-572-3993, or fax 317-572-4002. For technical support, please visit https://hub.wiley.com/community/support/dummies.

Wiley publishes in a variety of print and electronic formats and by print-on-demand. Some material included with standard print versions of this book may not be included in e-books or in print-on-demand. If this book refers to media such as a CD or DVD that is not included in the version you purchased, you may download this material at http://booksupport.wiley.com. For more information about Wiley products, visit www.wiley.com.

Library of Congress Control Number: 2022947689

ISBN: 978-1-119-93179-9 (pbk); ISBN 978-1-119-93181-2 (ebk); ISBN 978-1-119-93180-5 (ebk)

SKY10036294_102422

Contents at a Glance

Table of Contents

Introduction

A re you excited to discover how to use Instagram? We hope you are! Because we love Instagram, and we're excited to show you how to use it and how to have fun with it! Instagram is all about entertainment and creating enjoyable content. Because you've chosen this book, we know you're ready to get started creating an Instagram account you enjoy!

More and more people are joining Instagram every day. But with that growth comes a lot of noise and saturation from people who don't quite understand how to use the platform effectively. After reading this book, you'll have the tools and tactics necessary to build a successful Instagram profile.

About This Book

This book helps you use Instagram successfully. Instagram really is as simple as uploading a photo — and that was how the platform was initially designed. But you can do so many things with each photo or video — like adding filters, writing creative captions, and having conversations in the comments. And as Instagram adds more features to the platform, such as Reels, multi-image posts, and stories, understanding how to create additional content is just as important.

We take you through every step of setting up your profile, creating and uploading content to Instagram, writing descriptive captions, finding hashtags that help you get more exposure, adding new followers, and using all the fun features built into Instagram.

Foolish Assumptions

We made a few assumptions when writing this book. We assume that you

>> Have a smartphone

>> Have photos and videos you want to share

>> Don't want to look like an amateur, even if you're new to using Instagram

>> Are committed to devoting time and energy to build a presence on Instagram

>> Want to be a part of the Instagram community

If these assumptions are correct, then this book is for you! We're confident that the tactics and information in these pages will help you achieve your goals.

Icons Used in This Book

To make sure you don't miss important details, we use the following icons throughout this book. Here's what the different icons mean:

Anything marked with the Tip icon is a small piece of expert advice that will save you time and make your experience on Instagram easier.

This book is a reference, which means you don't have to commit it to memory. There won't be a test on Friday! But every once in a while, we tell you something so important that we think you should file it away with other important information, like your best friend's birthday and the name of the newest royal baby.

Most of this book is all about telling you what you need to know to use Instagram, and nothing more. But every once in a while, our inner geeks emerge, and we get a little technical. When this happens, we flag it with the Technical Stuff icon. If you're in a hurry, or you just don't care about this kind of thing, you can skip anything marked with the Technical Stuff icon without missing the point of the subject at hand.

WARNING

When you see a Warning icon, you're not at risk of blowing up your Instagram account or doing irreparable damage, but you can rest assured that some helpful advice is at hand — advice meant to prevent any headaches or minor snafus.

Beyond the Book

In addition to what you're reading right now, this book also comes with a free, access-anywhere Cheat Sheet that provides a handy list of Instagram lingo, size limits for photos and videos on Instagram, and steps for sharing posts and profiles. The Cheat Sheet also includes Instagram limits for everything from usernames to bios to the number of posts you can like in an hour. To view the Cheat Sheet, simply go to www.dummies.com and type **Instagram For Dummies Cheat Sheet** in the Search box.

Where to Go from Here

You don't have to read this book from beginning to end — in fact, you can use the Table of Contents and Index to find the information you're most interested in right this very minute. You don't even have to read every word. If you're short on time and just want to know what you need to know to get the job done, you can skip anything marked with the Technical Stuff icon, as well as sidebars (the text in gray boxes).

The first few chapters dive into how to set up a new Instagram account. If you already have an Instagram account, you can skip the first two chapters, but we encourage you to check out Chapter 2 because it contains information on how to set up an effective profile. Don't worry, you can easily update or edit anything you've already started! And if you're looking for inspiration, read Chapter 15.

TIP

Within this book, you may note that some web addresses break across two lines of text. If you're reading this book in print and want to visit one of these web pages, simply key in the web address exactly as it's noted in the text, pretending as though the line break doesn't exist. If you're reading this as an e-book, you've got it easy — just click the web address to be taken directly to the web page.

We would love to hear from you about your experience with this book. Did you find it helpful? Was there something else you wish we had covered? Are you enjoying using Instagram now? Please feel free to email us. You can reach Jenn at jenn@ jennstrends.com, Eric at eric@butow.net, and Corey at corey@ themarketingspecialist.com.

It's time to jump into all the fun of Instagram that we've been talking about! Enjoy the book!

1

Getting Started with Instagram

Chapter **1**

Setting Up Your Profile

After you install the Instagram app on your mobile device, the first major task you face is setting up your profile. Your profile should accurately represent you.

In this chapter, we show you how to set up the different components of your profile, including a username and name and a bio. We also explain how to set up a business profile, in case the account you're creating is for, well, a business. Finally, we end the chapter by showing you how to select your privacy settings.

Practicing Good Personal Profile Management

Instagram gives you the option of choosing between a personal or business profile. We start by explaining how to set up a personal profile. Later in this chapter, we discuss how to upgrade to a business profile.

TIP

If you want both a personal and a business profile, you can't do that in one account. You have to set up two separate accounts — one with a personal profile and another with a business profile.

Your Instagram profile is not only your first impression to potential followers and new visitors but also your consistent message to your existing audience. Your profile should be recognizable as your style and representative of what you want people to see about you. Figure 1-1 shows you what a standard personal profile looks like on Instagram.

FIGURE 1-1:
The Instagram profile consists of these standard components.

Instagram profiles are composed of the following six components: username, name, pronouns, profile photo, bio, and web address.

Choosing a username and name

Your username and name are two of the most important components of your Instagram profile because they help other users find you in search results. When users type a keyword or name in the Search field on Instagram, the app looks at the username and name fields of accounts to determine if an account is relevant to that search query.

Instagram also scans the caption text within your posts and your profile bio description to see whether your content appears in a user's search results when looking at keyword searches. If you want to get even more eyeballs to your profile, start adding keywords to your posts' captions and see what good things happen. We explain how to add captions in Chapter 3.

The username is the string of characters at the top of the profile. The name is the bold text below the profile photo. If you want your account to be found by a keyword or phrase, be sure to include it in either the name or username for your account.

Choosing the best username

When you set up a new Instagram account, you're required to choose a username. Your Instagram username is how you're recognized on Instagram: All activity, from the content you post to how you engage with others, is associated with your username. The username is at the top of the profile (refer to Figure 1-1).

Your username is delineated with the at (@) symbol when referring to you as a user. The web address (technically known as the *URL,* short for *Uniform Resource Locator*) for your Instagram account is

https://instagram.com/*yourusername*

When you interact on Instagram, the username appears as

yourusername

An Instagram username is limited to 30 characters and must contain only letters, numbers, periods, and underscores. You can't include symbols or other punctuation marks as a part of your username.

TIP

Choose a username that represents you or your name, is recognizable, and, if possible, distinguishes what you do. Your username may be simply your name or nickname. If you're already established on other social media, such as Twitter, you may want to choose the same username on Instagram as you use on other sites, so that your current audience can easily find you.

During the registration portion of your Instagram account, you're prompted to select your username. A check mark indicates whether the username you selected is available. If someone is using the username you entered, you see an X in the username field. Keep selecting alternatives until you find an available username.

TIP

If the username you want to use is unavailable, you can use alternative options by adding periods or underscores to the username, by using abbreviations, or by adding another word.

If you're signing up for a new Instagram account using the website, Instagram populates an available username for you. You're welcome to use this suggested name, but we don't recommend it because it's generic and won't represent you or be nearly as creative as one you come up with yourself.

You can also make a slogan your username or add a word in front of your name to differentiate yourself from a generic name. For example, a clothing boutique in Vancouver, British Columbia called Plenty has the word Get in front of their name, so their username is GetPlenty.

TIP

Always check what your username looks like as one long word. If you want your username to be "christopher u," it will appear as "christopheru," which may be misread as "chris to pheru," "christophe ru," or some other version. Instead, include an underscore or a period to separate words, like "christopher_u".

TECHNICAL STUFF

There is little you can do to have an existing username transferred to your account if it's in use or was previously registered by another user. If another account is using your registered trademark as its username, visit `https://help.instagram.`

com/101826856646059 for information on how to file a claim of trademark violation.

After you select a username, all content linking to your profile is associated with the username's URL. If you want to change the username at some point, your URL also changes, and you need to update all backlinks and links to that profile accordingly. This is why it's best to choose the right username when setting up your profile.

WARNING

If you have a verified Instagram account, you can't change your username without losing your verified status, which means the blue check won't appear next to your new username.

If you want to change your username, follow these steps (see Figure 1-2):

1. **Go to your profile on Instagram on either your mobile device or your computer.**

2. **Tap or click Edit Profile.**

3. **In the Username field, type the new username.**

4. **Save your changes.**

   To do so, tap the check mark, Done, Save, or Submit button (depending on the device you're using).

Choosing the best name

Your Instagram name is visible only when someone visits your profile directly or it appears in search results. The name appears in bold below the profile photo (refer to Figure 1-1). You can use your actual name or a nickname as your name on Instagram.

Your profile performs better in searches and looks less amateurish if the name and username are different. Having a name that's different from your username provides double the opportunity for keywords and searchable criteria in the Instagram app. Power users on Instagram take the time to craft good username and name components.

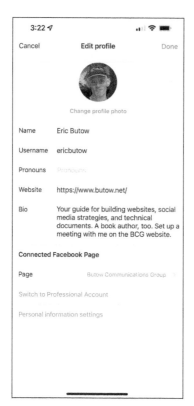

FIGURE 1-2:
Editing your
username
and name
information.

Unlike your username, which is one word, your name should be in proper sentence structure with capital letters and spacing. Your name (like your username) is limited to 30 characters, including spaces.

TIP

Avoid using a font generator to make your Instagram name look unique. These font generators allow you to create cursive fonts or block letters, but each letter is considered an emoji, not a character. Instagram doesn't consider those when "reading" the text of your name, so it diminishes your likelihood of appearing in search results.

TIP

You can be found in more searches on Instagram if you include a keyword or phrase in your name or username or both. If you don't put a defining keyword in your username, you should include one in your name field, in addition to your actual name.

The name on your profile is not tied to your URL or other defining aspects of Instagram, so you can change it without your username being affected. Consider adding or changing keywords, as necessary, to appeal to your target audience on Instagram.

If you want to change your name, do the following:

1. **Go to your Instagram profile, and tap or click Edit Profile.**

2. **In the Name field, type the new name.**

3. **Save your changes.**

   To do so, tap the check mark, Done, Save, or Submit button (depending on the device you're using).

Deciding on a profile photo

The *profile photo* on your account, as well as your username, is associated with all your activity. When you post anything to Instagram or engage with other users in any way, your profile photo is visible.

Your profile photo should represent you and be recognizable to others. If you actively use other social media platforms, you may want to use the same photograph for your Instagram profile as you already use on other platforms. That way, you create cohesion across your online media and assure your followers that they found the correct account when searching for you. The account of @cgritmon in Figure 1-3 is a good example of having a profile photo that stands out, is easy to recognize, and represents her as a person.

TIP

Profile photos on Instagram are cropped to a circle, so your photo should fit properly within that crop. Don't use a logo or an image that loses valuable content when cropped to a circle.

The profile photo on your profile page appears larger than anywhere else on Instagram. When interacting with others, the profile photo is a thumbnail (small) version. Choose an image that isn't too busy, overwhelming, or cluttered with text, which can make the image difficult to decipher as a thumbnail.

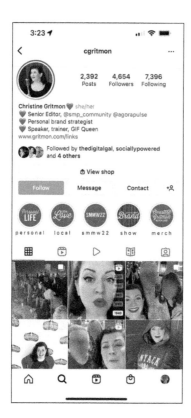

The best profile photos have a clear object of focus, contain a simple background, and are sized at least 550-x-550 pixels. The ideal image size is 1,080-x-1,080 pixels for a square image. (If you upload a photo that's too small, it may appear *pixelated*, which is what happens when a low-resolution image is enlarged too much and the individual square pixels become obvious, making the image blurry.)

Writing a Dazzling Bio

Your bio is a short description on your profile that tells people about you. This description is similar to a 30-second elevator pitch — it's how you convince new visitors to follow your account.

Most people read your bio only the first time they visit your profile. Your bio is the first impression you give to new viewers and should accurately convey the message you want to share.

Deciding what information to include

Before you start writing your bio, choose at least two or three key aspects of your life to highlight, such as the example shown in Figure 1-4. These should be traits that will connect emotionally, in some way, with those you want to attract.

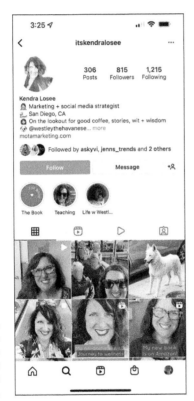

FIGURE 1-4:
A well-written bio attracts more followers.

You need to determine the voice and style of your bio. If you're the next Amy Schumer, your Instagram bio should reflect that irreverent, hilarious style through words and relevant emojis. In contrast, if your identity is more straitlaced and serious, your bio shouldn't be silly and humorous.

Even if your profile is meant to connect with friends and family, sharing your personality and purpose in the bio helps clarify that to people who may find you.

The Instagram bio is limited to 150 characters, including spaces. The bio is designed to be one single paragraph of information, but you can use formatting techniques to add spaces and line breaks.

TIP

Because Instagram was designed to be used on a mobile device, it's best to format your bio on a mobile device so that you retain the correct alignment.

Make use of emojis and symbols from your mobile device's keyboard to create visual appeal in your bio. To add emojis, open the emoji keyboard on your mobile device — just tap the smiley-face icon at the bottom of your keyboard.

TO HASHTAG OR NOT TO HASHTAG

Generally, hashtags are not a good idea in Instagram bios. Although they are clickable, if someone clicks the hashtag in your bio, they'll leave your profile and explore the hashtag gallery results instead. Using a hashtag like #photographer sends visitors from your profile to millions of other posts using that hashtag. Using hashtags in your bio is not a viable way to get more followers or showcase your own content.

You should only include hashtags in your bio if they're specific to you, your content, or your business. For example, if you recently got married and you had a hashtag for your wedding, you can include that hashtag in your bio so that anyone tapping on it will find all the other content created at your wedding.

Instagram is a visual platform, and having emojis in the bio helps yours stand out from other users'. You have many emojis to choose from. If the traditional funny face and cartoonish emojis don't translate to your style, use simple emoji symbols such as squares, diamonds, triangles, and arrows to add color and visual content without detracting from your professional style.

Formatting your bio

You can edit or create your bio by tapping the Edit Profile button in your Instagram profile. On the Edit Profile screen (refer to Figure 1-2), go to the Bio field and insert the text for your bio. Save any changes when you're finished.

Android users can format a bio completely in Instagram. If you want to include line breaks and spacing, tap the Return or Enter key (on the keyboard of your mobile device) at the end of the line. Make sure that you don't have an extra space after the final character on the line and that the last character on the line is not an emoji. If you have an extra space or an emoji as the final character, the space breaks you inserted with the Return or Enter key do not appear in your published text.

iOS users can format a bio in Instagram, but line breaks are not retained. Instead, it's best to open the Notes app on your device and use it to craft your bio description, including all formatting. Then copy the bio, open Instagram again, select Edit Profile, and paste the description in the Bio field. As with Android users, you must ensure that no extra space appears after the final character on the line and that the last character on the line is not an emoji.

TIP

You can edit and rewrite your bio as often as you want. We recommend reviewing your bio every six months to verify that the information is still accurate and relevant.

Considering layouts for your bio

Instagram has traditionally had the profile photo on the left side of the profile and the bio directly beneath it. As Instagram has added more features, like Reels and Story Highlights, the profile section has gotten longer and taken up more space. To alleviate this problem, Instagram began truncating the bios with a ". . . more" link as shown in Figure 1-5. Tapping the ". . . more" link opens the full bio.

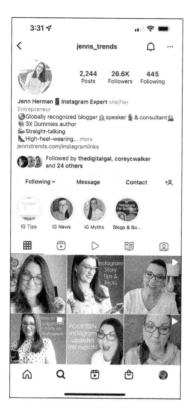

FIGURE 1-5: The "more" link in the bio appears just above the website link.

Adding a web address to your bio

Most people use web addresses in their bios when they're using their Instagram profiles for business purposes. But there may be occasions where you want to share a website link even on your personal profile.

Perhaps you want to send people to your YouTube videos, your personal gallery of photos on Flickr, or a reservation link for an upcoming party. In any of these situations, or others, you can include the URL for that destination in the link location in your bio.

The only place that you can place a clickable link on Instagram is in the bio and in stories. You can't include clickable links in regular posts. If you have any reason to send people to a website link, you need to place that link here in the bio.

From the Edit Profile button on your Instagram profile, there is the option to list a URL link. Simply copy and paste or type the link address in this field.

You can update or change your URL as frequently as you like. You may have a default web page for your profile but change it to coincide with a promotion or campaign you're running on Instagram. After that campaign is complete, you can change the link back to your default or simply delete it if you don't have anything to drive traffic to.

On a personal profile, you don't get Instagram analytics regarding how many people clicked the link in your bio. If you want to use this feature for business and drive traffic for your business, you should upgrade to a business profile on Instagram (see the next section, "Taking Advantage of a Business Profile Upgrade").

Taking Advantage of a Business Profile Upgrade

In late 2016, Instagram introduced business profiles. Before this feature rollout, all profiles on Instagram looked identical. Now brands have the capability to stand out from regular accounts and can benefit from a variety of features available only to business profiles.

By upgrading to a business profile on Instagram, you get features such as the following:

>> Easy-to-access contact buttons that make it easy for your customers to email you, call you, order food, book an appointment, reserve a table, or get directions to your location

>> An industry listing that informs visitors what you do as a business

>> In-app analytics to best monitor what is and isn't working in your content strategy

>> The ability to boost posts from your Instagram profile and run ads on Instagram

>> The ability to manage your Instagram comments and engagement through your Facebook page

REMEMBER

You're allowed only one clickable link (in your bio). The contact button feature means people can call, text, or email you, or get directions to your business location, providing you additional ways to connect directly with your customers and close more sales!

To upgrade to a business profile, do the following:

1. **Log in to Instagram on your mobile device and tap Edit Profile.**

2. **Tap the Switch to Professional Account option (see Figure 1-6).**

3. **Choose Business and follow the prompts to select your Category and email contact info.**

4. **If you have a Facebook page to connect your account to, select it from the Pages you're logged into. If you don't have a Facebook page, tap Don't Connect to Facebook Now.**

5. **Update or add information as necessary.**

   For example, if your information does not populate a phone number but you would like to include the Call contact button, you can add your phone number to that field in the Contact Options screen.

   You can edit this information at any time in case you want to add or delete a contact option later.

6. **Save your information.**

   Tap the check mark in the upper-right corner of the Contact Options screen.

FIGURE 1-6:
Upgrade to
a business
profile by
selecting the
Switch to
Professional
Account
option.

Your Instagram account is now set up as a business profile! After upgrading your account, your new business profile appears to anyone visiting your profile.

REMEMBER

Even though you have these additional features as a business profile, your profile characteristics, such as your username, name, bio, and URL, remain the same.

TECHNICAL STUFF

Instead of a Business account, you can also opt to have a Creator account. This type of account has similar features to a Business account, including options for insights and analytics, but does not currently cooperate with third-party tools, so you won't be able to use a scheduling tool or social media management tool to manage your Instagram account if you have a Creator account. Instagram gears its Creator account to content creators, public figures, photographers, artists, and influencers.

Modifying Your Account Privacy Settings

When you set up a new Instagram account, it defaults to a public account, meaning anyone on Instagram can find you and see your content. Many Instagram users are okay with this, but if you want to keep your account more private, you can.

When your account is private, other users are able to see your username, name, profile photo, and bio, but they can't see any of your posts.

To edit your privacy settings, follow these steps (see Figure 1-7):

1. Go to your Instagram profile and tap the three-line button in the upper-right corner.

2. Tap Settings at the bottom of the screen.

3. Tap Privacy.

4. Tap the toggle button for the option to make your account private.

When you make these changes, anyone who is currently following you doesn't see anything different on your profile, but anyone who is not currently following you can no longer see your account posts. If someone wants to follow you, they need to request to follow you. You receive that request, and you can approve or deny that person the ability to follow you.

IN THIS CHAPTER

» Discovering what's in your feed

» Figuring out the Instagram algorithm

» Managing all three Instagram feeds

» Finding new accounts that interest you

» Looking at notifications and what they mean

Chapter **2**

Navigating Instagram

After you've installed Instagram and set up your Instagram profile, it's time to start seeing what Instagram is all about! There are millions of accounts waiting for you to explore. You'll be amazed at the variety and specificity available to you with just a few taps on your mobile phone. Are you a fan of Australian shepherds? There are 2 million posts about them. Like azaleas? You'll find more than 188,000 posts out there waiting for you! Not to mention all the people who may become part of your online tribe when you find you have similar interests (or even if you don't).

In this chapter, we explain what's in your feed and how the Instagram algorithm decides what to show you. Next, we talk about how to manage Instagram's three-feed function so you can see updates from your regular feed as well as from your followers and your favorites. Then we fill you in on the Explore page and the variety of different ways to search for people, hashtags, and places. Finally, you get the skinny on your notifications and what you should do with them.

Scrolling through the Feed

If you're familiar with other social media platforms, like Facebook or Twitter, you're probably used to having a "feed." You get to the Instagram feed by tapping the house at the lower-left corner of your screen, as shown in Figure 2-1. There, you can scroll through to see posts from the accounts and hashtags you're following (plus ads and accounts Instagram suggests). However, it's important to note that the Instagram feed is extremely personalized for each individual user. Even if two people followed the exact same accounts, they would get different feeds because they would interact with the content from those accounts in different ways. You can find out more about the way content is shown to you when we talk about the Instagram algorithm in the next section.

FIGURE 2-1: The Instagram feed is accessed by tapping the house at the lower-left corner of your screen.

Your feed is the hub of your interactions with people. It allows you to access the following (see Figure 2-2):

A. New Instagram stories from the people you follow at the very top of your feed

B. Posts from the people and hashtags you follow, ads, and suggested posts from Instagram

C. The ability to create new Instagram stories by tapping the plus icon at the upper right of the screen and then tapping Story in the drop-down menu, or by swiping right on any post in your feed

D. The ability to create a Reel by tapping the plus icon at the upper right of the screen and then tapping Reel in the drop-down menu, or by swiping right and selecting Reel at the bottom of the screen

E. The ability to create a new post by tapping the plus icon at the upper right of the screen and then tapping Post in the drop-down menu

F. Notifications by tapping the heart at the upper right of the screen

G. Direct messages by tapping the speech bubble (with a lightning bolt inside it) at the upper right of the screen

H. The Explore page by tapping the magnifying glass at the lower left of the screen

I. The Reels page by tapping the Reels icon in the bottom center of the screen

J. The Shop page by tapping the shopping bag at the lower right of the screen

K. Your profile by tapping your profile photo at the lower far right of the screen

FIGURE 2-2:
Your
Instagram
feed gives
you access
to all
areas of
Instagram.

Making Sense of the Instagram Algorithm

Ahhhh, the mysterious Instagram algorithm. Everyone has a theory about the way it works, but Instagram finally shared how content is ranked in each user's feed in 2018. Instagram uses four major factors to determine what's shown:

>> **Reels:** The algorithm favors Reels above all other content. Why, you ask? One word: TikTok, Instagram's archrival. (Okay, that was three words.)

>> **Interest:** Instagram is looking at the content you interact with to determine what you want more of. If you always like or comment on content from certain accounts, that's a high level of interest. If you always like a certain type of content (like dogs or cars or food), then more of that type of content will appear higher in your feed. (Yes, Instagram uses artificial intelligence and other factors to determine what's in the content and determine whether you have an interest in it.) Similarly, if you always watch videos, video content will rank higher in your feed than photos or graphic images. Interest or relevancy is based on the prediction of how likely you are to actually interact with the content placed in front of you.

>> **Timeliness:** The recency of the posts from those you follow is an important factor in what you see. Instagram puts more emphasis on recency of posts to ensure you see content that is fresher.

>> **Relationships:** Instagram cares about who you interact with the most. Which accounts do you always comment on or "like" the posts of? Or which accounts do you regularly visit via their profiles? These indicators mean you probably really want to see their content, and chances are, these people are your friends or family, so their content appears higher in your feed.

A few other factors play into the algorithm, such as the following:

>> **Frequency:** How often you use Instagram and log in determines how much of the content in your feed gets sorted. For example, if you log in every hour, not a lot of content needs to be sorted. So it looks fairly chronological, and you see pretty much everything. But if you only log in once a week, a ton of content has been uploaded by everyone you follow, so that content gets some serious ranking and sorting to put the most relevant content at the top of your feed, and you may not see every post from everyone you follow.

>> **Following:** Obviously, if you follow more accounts, that means there's a lot more content in your feed. The more content there is, the more it's sorted and ranked. So, following fewer people means you see more stuff from the people you care most about.

>> **Usage:** This ties into both of the preceding points. If you're on Instagram for hours a day, the algorithm digs further into the content sources to give you fresh content at the top of your feed. If, however, you only log on for ten minutes a day, you're just going to see the highlights that Instagram thinks are most relevant to you. It's like watching the evening news: If you watch the first five minutes, you get all the day's highlights. But if you keep watching the whole broadcast, you get all the stories and the juicy little extras they throw in throughout the full program.

Managing Not One, Not Two, but Three Feeds!

As we started writing the new edition of this book, Instagram rolled out its three-feed function. Every time you log into Instagram, you see your regular feed, but you can manually view content from your favorite Instagram users or see all the posts of those you follow in chronological order.

It's not obvious on the screen, but when you tap the Instagram logo in the upper-left corner of the screen, you see a down arrow to the right of the logo and a drop-down menu that enables you to view either the Favorites or Following tabs. The Favorites tab is only the content of those you've added to this list. The Following tab is the chronological feed of all those you follow.

TIP

If you don't have any favorites, then the Favorites screen invites you to add your favorites.

The Favorites feed works a lot like lists in Twitter or other apps where you can selectively choose to see updates from only a select group of users. This is great for keeping up-to-date with just your friends or family, experts in your career industry, or local hobby enthusiasts with similar interests to you.

When you're in the Favorites or Following feeds, return to your regular feed by tapping the arrow beside Favorites or Following in the upper-left corner of the screen.

Exploring the World of Instagram

If you're having trouble finding all the accounts you want to follow, Instagram has a solution for you. The Explore page offers photo and video posts, shopping posts, and Reels all tailored to you by the algorithm. It factors in accounts you're already following and interacting with, and shows you content that is similar or related in the hopes that you'll tap on it.

Finding and viewing the Explore page

Here's how to use the Explore page:

1. **Tap the magnifying glass at the bottom of any screen.**

   Several photos and Reels are presented, as shown in Figure 2-3.

2. **Tap any photo or video that interests you.**

   Now you can scroll down to see the rest of the Explore page.

3. **If you'd like to see more posts from an account, tap the Instagram username at the top of any post that interests you.**

4. **Look around the page. If you want to follow that account, tap the Follow button at the top of the user's profile page.**

FIGURE 2-3:
The Explore
page
displays
posts you
may like.
You can also
search by
topic using
the buttons
at the top of
the Explore
page.

Searching for what makes you happy

Another great way to find new content is by using the Explore page to search Instagram. To try out the Search feature, tap the magnifying glass on any page. The Explore page appears, as described in the preceding section. Tap the Search field at the top of the page.

Below the Search field, a row of small boxes appears containing search terms suggested by Instagram (see Figure 2-4). Swipe left and right within the row to see if there's a topic that strikes your fancy. If so, tap on the term's box to open the Explore page for that topic.

FIGURE 2-4:
At the top of the screen, search by typing text in the Search field or tap a topic box.

TIP

When you open a new Explore page for a topic, you may see subtopic boxes at the top of the screen. For example, if you tap the home office topic, the Explore page shows subtopic suggestions including furniture and (importantly) coffee. Tap that subtopic to view the Explore page for that subtopic.

Checking Your Notifications

If you participate regularly on Instagram, posting content, following new people, making comments and more, you'll start getting notifications. You access notifications by tapping the heart at the upper right of your screen while on any page within the main Instagram app (not stories).

The notifications shown on the Activity page (see Figure 2-5) are from people who have recently

>> Followed you

>> Liked one of your posts

>> Commented on one of your posts, stories, or Reels

>> Tagged you in a post

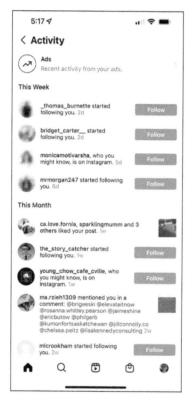

FIGURE 2-5:
Notifications appear in reverse chronological order on the Activity page.

TIP

If you've been on Instagram a while, you'll also get notifications for Memories that say, "On this Day." Clicking the thumbnail opens the old post in Instagram stories so you can share it.

To go to a new follower's account, tap their name from the Activity page.

To see the post that someone liked, commented on, or tagged you on, tap the thumbnail of the photo from the Activity page.

If you scroll further down the page, Instagram suggests other people to follow that the algorithm deems interesting to you.

TIP

You can get push notifications on your phone if you'd like to see who's commenting and liking your page in real time. To turn on Push Notifications, follow these steps:

1. **Go to your profile and tap the three lines at the top right of the screen.**

2. **Tap Settings.**

3. **Tap Notifications and choose which activities you'd like to get notifications about, or use the Pause All slider to stop getting any push notifications.**

2

Getting Creative with Instagram Content

Master the art of taking great photos.

Discover the best video-making tactics.

Chapter **3**

Taking and Posting Great Photos

n this chapter, you find out how to take photos with Instagram, use editing tools to make your photos look their best, and then share photos stored on your iPhone, iPad, or Android smartphone or tablet with your followers and on other social networks.

REMEMBER

You can upload photos only in the Instagram app on your smartphone or tablet, not from the Instagram website.

All figures in this chapter were taken using the iPhone app because that's Instagram's native platform. Don't worry, Android users — we note any differences between the iPhone and Android apps throughout.

Taking Your Best Shot

Before you can post a photo on Instagram, you need to tell the app where to get the photo. In this section, we cover taking a photo. For details on selecting from your existing photos, see the "Uploading Photos from Your Camera Roll" section, later in this chapter.

When you first log in to Instagram, you see your feed on the screen. Tap the plus (+) icon at the top of the home screen and then tap Post in the drop-down menu. When prompted, allow Instagram access to your phone's camera. (The good news is that you have to go through this process only once. The next time you open Instagram and tap the plus (+) icon, you won't have to enable camera access.)

REMEMBER

You can also take a photo in a post by swiping right in the feed screen. The camera screen allows you to create a photo in a story by default. (Read more about creating and publishing stories starting in Chapter 7.) In the camera screen, add a photo to a post by tapping Post at the bottom of the screen, below the shutter button.

Next, you see the New Post screen. Tap the Camera icon shown in Figure 3-1.

Now you see the Photo screen shown in Figure 3-2. Note the following elements in the camera screen:

>> **Viewer:** View the object or person where your camera is aimed. The viewer takes up most of the real estate on the screen.

>> **Switch cameras icon:** Tap the icon to switch between your smartphone's front and back cameras.

>> **Camera settings:** Tap this icon to see the Camera Settings screen where you can set camera controls as well as change settings for a story, reel, or live broadcast.

— Tap to take a photo for a post.

>> **Flash icon:** Tap the flash icon to toggle the following flash modes:

- **Off:** This mode is the default. The lightning bolt icon has a line through it.

- **On:** The lightning bolt icon has no line through it.

- **Auto-detect:** The lightning bolt icon has an *A* next to it.

>> **Shutter button:** Tap the shutter button to take a picture.

>> **Recents icon:** Tap this icon to view and select recent photos stored on your device.

>> **Cancel button (iOS) or X (Android):** Tap this button to return to your Instagram feed.

When you're ready to take a photo, tap the shutter button.

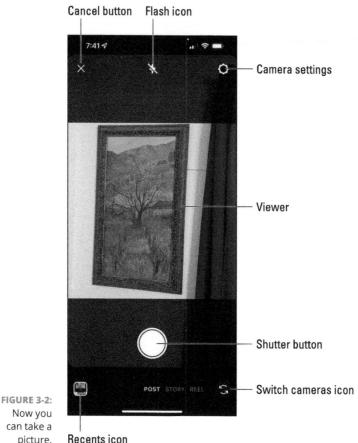

Cancel button   Flash icon

Camera settings

Viewer

Shutter button

Switch cameras icon

FIGURE 3-2:
Now you
can take a
picture.   Recents icon

Improving Your Best Shot

The photo you've just taken appears in the viewer of the Filter screen, as shown in Figure 3-3. The screen contains the following four sections, from top to bottom:

» **Top menu bar:** This menu bar has a < (back) icon on the left, the Lux icon in the center (which you find out more about later in this chapter), and the Next link on the right.

» **Viewer:** The viewer displays your photo.

>> **Filter thumbnail images:** This row of images lets you see what your photo will look like with a filter applied.

>> **Bottom menu bar:** This menu bar has a Filter menu option (selected by default) and the Edit option.

FIGURE 3-3:
The Filter
screen.

TIP

Not interested in editing your photo? Simply tap Next in the upper-right corner of the Filter screen shown in Figure 3-3 to move to the next editing stage.

Applying a filter

Below your photo in the viewer is a row of filters. Each filter includes a thumbnail image so you can see the filter's effect on your photo.

Swipe from right to left in the row of thumbnail images to view all 23 filters, from Clarendon to Nashville. (Normal is the default image, without a filter.) Tap a filter thumbnail image, and the photo in the viewer changes to show you the photo with that filter applied.

To return to the original photo, tap the Normal thumbnail (refer to Figure 3-3). To continue processing the photo with a filter, either tap Edit at the lower-right corner of the screen to edit your photo further or tap Next in the upper-right corner of the screen to add a description to your photo. (You find out how to add a description in the "Enriching Your Photo" section, later in this chapter.)

What happens when a filter is not quite to your liking and you'd like to tweak it? You can change the intensity of any filter (except Normal) by tapping the filter thumbnail image again. A slider appears; move it to the left or right to change the intensity. The photo in the viewer changes to reflect the selected intensity. The default intensity for each filter is 100.

When you've set the intensity to just the right amount, tap Done (iOS) or the check mark (Android). If you're still not satisfied and want to return the photo to its original intensity, tap Cancel (iOS) or the X (Android).

If you want to see how the photo with a filter compares to the original photo, tap and hold down on the viewer to view the original photo. Release your finger to see the photo with the applied filter.

Tweaking with the editing tools

When you've finished experimenting with filters, view Instagram's editing tools by tapping Edit (iOS) or Edit/Filter (Android) at the bottom of the screen. A row of editing tools appears below the viewer, as shown in Figure 3-4.

FIGURE 3-4:
The tool
name
appears
above each
tool icon.

Swipe from right to left in the row of editing tools to see all 13 tools. Tap a tool to open it below the viewer.

What you see below the viewer depends on the tool you tapped. For example, when you tap the Brightness tool, a slider appears so you can increase or decrease the photo's brightness. No matter what tool you use, the photo in the viewer reflects the changes you make and a gray dot appears below the tool icon.

Here are the various editing tools built into Instagram. Tapping any of these enables you to edit that component of the photo:

» Adjust

» Brightness

» Contrast

» Structure

- » Warmth

- » Saturation

- » Color

- » Fade

- » Highlights

- » Shadows

- » Vignette

- » Tilt Shift

- » Sharpen

TIP

You can change the photo perspective using the slider bar in the Adjust screen (refer to Figure 3-5). You can change the color of your photo shadow by tapping the color dot, as shown in Figure 3-6.

FIGURE 3-5: Use the slider bar in the Adjust screen to change the photo's perspective.

FIGURE 3-6:
Tap the color dot to select a color for your photo shadow.

After you finish making changes to your photo, apply your effect by tapping Done (iOS) or the check mark (Android). Or discard the effect by tapping Cancel (iOS) or the X (Android).

Saving your changes (or not)

When you've finished using the editing tools and filters, you can do one of three things:

>> **Discard your changes** and return to the Photo screen by tapping the left arrow icon in the upper-left corner and then tapping Discard in the pop-up menu.

>> **Save your changes and continue editing** by tapping the left arrow icon and then tapping Save Draft in the pop-up menu. Then Instagram takes you back to the camera screen, not your photo, so you'll have to select the photo in your library to continue editing it.

>> **Add a description** to the photo by tapping Next in the upper-right corner. The New Post screen appears, where you can add a caption and location, tag friends, and decide whether you want to share the photo on other social networks (see the next section).

To follow along with the example in this chapter, tap Next.

Enriching Your Photo

After you tap Next on the Edit screen, the New Post screen appears, as shown in Figure 3-7. On this screen, you can add a caption to your photo, tag people who appear in the photo, include the photo's location, share the photo on other social media networks, and turn commenting on and off.

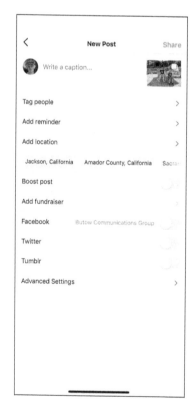

FIGURE 3-7: Add details to your photo here.

Describing your photo

To add a description to your photo, tap in the top section where it says "Write a caption. . . ." A keyboard appears at the bottom of the screen.

REMEMBER

Captions can't exceed 2,200 characters. You'll know you've reached the limit when you keep typing and no characters appear in the caption box.

When you've finished writing, tap OK (iOS) or Share (Android) in the upper-right corner of the screen. The text of your caption appears in the caption box.

To edit the caption, tap in the caption box and make your changes. When you're finished, tap OK.

It's good to have options

Below the caption box are options to do lots of good stuff:

>> Identify people and products in your photo

>> Add a reminder for your event promoted in your post

>> Add a location to your photo

>> Add a fundraiser to your post and bio so you can draw attention to a nonprofit organization you support

>> Share your photo on other social networks

>> Turn commenting on and off (under the Advanced Settings link at the bottom)

Tagging people

When you *tag* people, you add their Instagram usernames to your photo so they know that you posted a photo with them in it. Instagram enables you to tag up to 20 people in a single photo. To tag a person in your photo, do the following:

1. **On the New Post screen, tap Tag People.**

   The Tag People screen appears.

2. **Tap the photo to tag.**

   The Search screen appears.

3. **In the Search for a Name box, type the username of the person you want to tag, and then tap the Search key in the keyboard.**

   A list of people appears below the box.

4. **Swipe up and down in the list until you find the person you want to tag, and then tap the person's name.**

   You can tag only people who appear in the list.

5. **Repeat this process to tag more people.**

6. **When you've finished tagging people, tap Done in the upper-right corner of the screen.**

WARNING

Be sure that you tag only people who are in the photo. Fortunately, if you tag someone by mistake, you can tap on the tag and then click the X that appears to the right of the person's name. But if you go ahead and tag someone who isn't in the photo, the tagged person may report you to Instagram, and then you may be subject to "deleted content, disabled accounts, or other restrictions" per Instagram's Community Guidelines. However, if the photo contains a logo or product, you can tag the brand or company associated with the product or logo.

Adding your location

You can include your current location in the photo's description. Tap Add Location. Your smartphone or tablet asks if the Instagram app can use your location if it's the first time you are adding a location. Tap Allow in the pop-up window to continue.

On the Locations screen that appears, swipe up and down in the list of nearby locations. If you can't find your location, tap the Search box at the top of the screen and start typing. As you type, results that most closely match your search term(s) appear in the list. When you find the location in the list, tap the location name.

If you want to delete the location, tap the delete icon (X) to the right of the location. After you delete the location, you see Add Location again on the screen.

REMEMBER

After you allow the Instagram app to use your location, the next time you open the New Post screen, you'll see a row of potential locations below Add Location. Swipe up in the row to view more locations. Tap the location name to select it as your location. You can still add a location by tapping Add Location and either selecting a location from the list or by typing the location in the Search box and then selecting the location in the list.

TIP

Post options depend on the type of account you have. For example, if you have a professional or creator account, you'll see an option for boosting your post with ads.

Facebook

Tap the dot to toggle the Facebook switch from left to right to log into Facebook and post your photo to your Facebook news-feed, as well as to Instagram. If this is the first time you're posting to Facebook, you have to allow Facebook to access your Instagram account.

TIP

The post is shared with your Facebook friends or on your Facebook page — whichever account you've connected to your Instagram account.

Twitter

If you want to tweet the same Instagram photo you're preparing, tap the dot to toggle the Twitter switch from left to right to log into your Twitter account. After you log in, you can share your photo and caption in a tweet. Remember that Twitter cuts off any caption that exceeds 280 characters. If this is the first time you're posting to Twitter from Instagram, you have to allow Twitter access to your account.

You have to tap the toggle dot every time you want to share on Twitter.

Tumblr

You can post your photo to your Tumblr account by tapping the Tumblr dot to toggle from left to right. Tumblr opens so you can log into your account, and then you return to Instagram. When you share your photo and related information in Instagram, you share it to your Tumblr feed as well.

You have to tap the toggle dot every time you want to share on Tumblr.

Turning commenting on and off

Before you share your photo, you may not want to take the time to read or respond to comments. You can block your followers from leaving comments about your photo. Begin by tapping the Advanced Settings option at the bottom of the New Post screen (refer to Figure 3-7). In the Advanced Settings screen, tap the Turn Off Commenting dot to toggle from left to right. To return to the New Post screen, tap the left arrow in the upper-left corner.

Posting Your Photos: Ta Da!

Your photo or photos are now ready to share with the Instagram world, so all you have to do is tap Share on iOS devices (refer to Figure 3-7) or the check mark on Android devices in the upper-right corner of the New Post screen.

After you post a photo, the home screen appears with your photo at the top, as shown in Figure 3-8. If you've posted several photos in one post, you'll be able to swipe in your post to view them all.

FIGURE 3-8:
Your photo
appears in
your news
feed.

Uploading Photos from Your Camera Roll

Do you have some photos you've already shot that you'd like to share with your followers? It's easy to select one or more photos and then share them on your Instagram feed. Here's how to upload photos from your camera:

1. **Tap the plus (+) icon at the top of the home screen.**

2. **Tap Post in the drop-down menu.**

   The New Post screen appears with the Recents section in the bottom half of the screen as shown in Figure 3-9. (Android users see the Gallery screen.) The most recent photo you saved to your smartphone appears in the viewer. Thumbnail-size photos appear below the viewer.

3. **Swipe through the thumbnail photos to view other photos. When you find one you like, tap it.**

   The selected photo appears in the viewer. Instagram automatically crops your photo to the size of the viewer.

4. **Tap Next.**

5. **(Optional) Apply filters and edit your photo as described earlier.**

6. **Tap Next.**

   The New Post screen appears.

7. **(Optional) Write a caption, tag people, add a location, change advanced settings and recipients, and share your photo on other social networks.**

   For details, bookmark this page and read the earlier section, "Enriching Your Photo."

8. **When you're ready to share your photos, tap Share on iOS or the check mark on Android devices.**

FIGURE 3-9:
The thumbnail of the selected photo appears dimmed.

Uploading Multiple Photos to One Post

You don't need to have one post for each photo. Instead, you can add as many as ten photos from your Camera Roll (or Gallery if you use an Android smartphone) to a single post.

Selecting multiple photos

To choose more than one photo to add to a post, do the following:

1. **In the main Instagram feed screen, tap the plus (+) icon at the top of the screen.**

2. **Tap Post in the drop-down menu.**

   The most recent photo in your Camera Roll appears at the top of the viewer with the Recents section of thumbnail photos underneath.

3. **Swipe through the thumbnail photos and tap the first photo you want to add.**

4. **Tap the select multiple icon that contains overlapped rounded squares; the highlighted icon in blue appears above the list of thumbnail images shown in Figure 3-10.**

   The selected thumbnail appears dimmed, with a blue number 1, as shown in Figure 3-10.

5. **Tap another thumbnail.**

   The photo appears in the viewer, and a number 2 appears next to the thumbnail. That number shows you the order in which your followers will see the photos in your post.

REMEMBER

   If you select a photo but then decide that you don't want to include it, just tap the thumbnail photo. The order of your photos changes if you select more than two photos. To deselect all photos, tap the blue select multiple icon in the lower-right corner of the viewer.

6. **Continue tapping thumbnails as needed.**

   In Figure 3-11, we've chosen three photos. The numbers reflect the order in which we selected each photo.

7. **When you've finished selecting photos, tap Next.**

The Edit screen appears.

Select Multiple icon

FIGURE 3-10:
The select
multiple
icon in the
viewer
appears in
blue above
the
upper-right
thumbnail
image in the
list.

Edit the photos by tapping Next in the upper-right corner of the screen.

TIP

To reorder the thumbnail photos in the New Post screen, you have to deselect them and then reselect them in the correct order. (Yes, this is something Instagram needs to work on.) For example, suppose you select five photos and want to move photos 3 and 4 to positions 4 and 5, respectively. First, deselect photos 3 and 4. At this point, the former photo 5 becomes photo 3. Then select the former photo 3, which becomes photo 4, and then select the former photo 4, which becomes photo 5.

FIGURE 3-11:
The most
recently
selected
photo
appears in
the viewer.

Applying filters and adding photos

After you have selected your photos and tapped Next, the Edit screen appears, as shown in Figure 3-12. The top of the screen displays the photo you're editing.

A row of filter types appears below the photo. Swipe from right to left in the row to view all the filters. To apply a filter to all photos in the group, tap the thumbnail image under the filter name.

TIP

You can apply a filter to only one photo in the group by tapping on a photo and then applying a filter and edits. When you're finished, tap Done in the upper-right corner of the screen. Feel free to have different filters and edits for every photo in your post!

FIGURE 3-12:
The filter
name
appears
above the
filter
thumbnail
image.

At the right side of the screen, you see part of the next photo in your photo group. To see the other photos, swipe left. To add another photo to your post, swipe to the end of the row, tap the plus (+) icon, and then select the photo from the Camera Roll screen, as described in the "Uploading Photos from Your Camera Roll" section earlier in this chapter.

Editing photos individually

To edit a photo, tap it in the row of photos. The selected photo appears in the center of your screen. Now you can do the following:

>> **Add a filter.** Swipe right to left in the filter row, and then tap the filter thumbnail image. Get all the details in the "Adding a filter" section.

>> **Change the exposure and brightness levels at once.** Tap the Lux icon (half-light, half-dark sun) at the top of the screen. Find out more about using the Lux tool in the section "Tweaking with the editing tools."

>> **Perform other editing tasks.** Tap Edit, and then follow the instructions in the "Tweaking with the editing tools" section.

Tap Done in the upper-right corner when you're finished.

Adding information and sharing your photos

When your photos are the way you want them, tap Next in the upper-right corner of the Edit screen.

In the New Post screen, you can write a caption, tag people, add a location, share your photo on other social networks, and turn commenting on and off as described earlier in the "Enriching Your Photo" section.

TIP

You can't write a caption for each photo when you have multiple photos in your post. So when you write your description, the caption should describe all your photos, not just one.

When you've finished editing your photos, it's time to share them. Tap Share in the upper-right corner of the New Post screen.

IN THIS CHAPTER

» Recording video on your smartphone or tablet

» Getting your videos ready to post

» Posting your video

» Posting multiple videos from an iPhone or iPad

» Uploading longer videos from your computer desktop

Chapter **4**

Recording and Posting Great Videos

Your iPhone, iPad, and Android devices all have video cameras, and Instagram puts them to great use. In this chapter, we explain how to record, edit, and share video in the Instagram app by using a smartphone or a tablet. Sorry, Windows users: Instagram doesn't support using your webcam to take video.

Recording Videos

Instagram gives you the flexibility to record or upload videos in posts on mobile devices that are as short as 1 second or as long as 60 seconds. If you find that 60 seconds is too limiting, use the video as a teaser (think of it as your own movie preview) to get people to click through to your website or to another video website such as YouTube.

When you're ready to start recording a video on your iPhone, iPad, Android smartphone, or Android tablet, open the Instagram app (if it's not open already) and then tap the plus (+) icon at the top of the home screen. Then tap Post in the drop-down menu.

REMEMBER

The Instagram apps on the iPhone, iPad, Android smartphones, and Android tablets all work the same.

The first time you open the Camera screen, a pop-up window appears, as shown in Figure 4-1. Instagram wants to access the microphone on your smartphone so it can record videos with sound. Access the microphone by tapping OK.

REMEMBER

You can also take a video in a post by swiping right in the feed screen. The camera screen allows you to create a video in a story by default, and you can find out more about creating and publishing stories starting in Chapter 7. You can also take a video in a reel; you find more about reels in Part 5. In the camera screen, add a video to a post by tapping Post at the bottom of the screen.

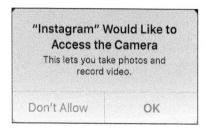

FIGURE 4-1:
If you want
to record
silent videos,
tap Don't
Allow.

"Instagram" Would Like to
Access the Camera

This lets you take photos and
record video.

Don't Allow   OK

REMEMBER

The next time you open the camera screen, you won't see this pop-up window. If you want to turn your microphone off and on in Instagram, access your smartphone's settings, open the Instagram settings, and then turn the microphone on or off.

The camera screen has the following elements, all labeled in Figure 4-2:

>> **Viewer:** The viewer appears in the center area of the screen.

>> **Switch cameras icon:** Tap the icon to switch between your smartphone's front and back cameras.

» **Camera Settings:** When you tap this icon, the Camera Settings screen appears so you can set camera controls as well as change settings for a story, reel, or live broadcast.

» **Flash icon:** Tap the flash icon to toggle the following flash modes:

- **Off:** This mode is the default. The lightning bolt icon has a line through it.

- **On:** The lightning bolt icon has no line through it.

- **Auto-detect:** The lightning bolt icon has an *A* next to it.

» **Shutter button:** The shutter button is what you tap to take a picture.

» **Cancel button (iOS) or X (Android):** Tap this button to return to your Instagram feed.

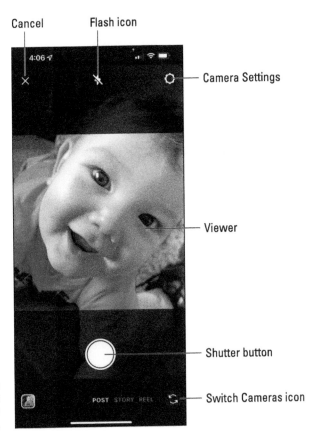

Cancel   Flash icon

Camera Settings

Viewer

Shutter button

FIGURE 4-2:
Now you can take a video.

Switch Cameras icon

When you're ready to take a video, tap and hold the shutter button. The orange-red recording bar appears as a circle around the shutter button as you record your video (see Figure 4-3).

FIGURE 4-3:
The orange-red recording bar grows as you record the video.

Once you release your finger or after you've recorded 60 seconds of video, the video plays continuously in the viewer within the Filter screen. You can pause playback by tapping anywhere in the viewer. When you want to play it again, tap the Play button, in the middle of the viewer, as shown in Figure 4-4.

TIP

You can toggle video sound on or off by tapping the speaker icon at the top of the page. If you've stopped your video, the video starts playing after you turn the video sound on or off.

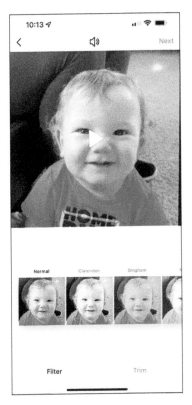

FIGURE 4-4:
Begin
playing the
video by
tapping the
Play button.

Improving Your Video

You can improve your video in several ways: by adding a filter, changing the cover frame, and trimming the video. In this section, you start by applying a filter to your video in the Filter screen.

Applying a filter

Below the viewer is a row of filters. (The Normal, Clarendon, and Gingham filters are shown in Figure 4-4.) The thumbnail image below each filter shows you the filter's effect on your video.

Swipe in the row of thumbnails to view all 23 filters. (Normal is the default, so it isn't considered a filter.) Tap a filter's thumbnail, and the video with the applied filter plays in the viewer.

You can change the intensity of any filter by tapping the filter's thumbnail and then moving the slider to the left or right. (The default intensity is 100.) As you move the slider, the video reflects the change. When you've finished selecting an intensity, tap Done.

REMEMBER

The video continues to play (or starts to play if the video is paused) when you apply a new filter or change the intensity of a filter. If you want to return the video to its original state, tap the Normal thumbnail.

Trimming to fit

If you find your video is too long, tap Trim at the lower-right corner of the Filter screen shown in Figure 4-4. The Trim screen shown in Figure 4-5 plays the video in the viewer at the top of the screen and has the timeline with all the frames in the video underneath the viewer.

FIGURE 4-5: The timeline is in a white box at the bottom of the screen.

As the video plays, the white bar in the timeline moves from left to right to denote the video frame that's playing. You can remove frames in the video by tapping and holding the white resizing bars on each end of the timeline and then dragging the bar to the left and right.

Frames that aren't playing appear dimmed, but you can view them again by dragging the resizing bars to the left or right. As you move the resizing bars, the video plays so you can see how the video looks without the frames you hid.

When you're happy with your trim and filter, tap Next in the upper-right corner of the screen.

Changing the cover frame

Instagram uses the first frame from your video to produce a *cover frame*, which is the frame that appears at the start of your video and in your Instagram feed. You can change the cover frame as follows:

1. **On the New Post screen, tap Cover in the upper-left corner of the screen.**

   The default cover frame appears in the viewer and also below the viewer in a white focus box. The other frames appear next to the focus box and are dimmed, as shown in Figure 4-6.

2. **Tap and hold down on the frame in the focus box, and then drag the frame within the row.**

   As you drag, the focus box moves to another frame in your video, and you see this new cover frame in the viewer.

3. **When you find a cover frame you like, release your finger.**

4. **Tap Done.**

TIP

The cover frame will appear in your Instagram feed, so be sure that the frame you select isn't blurry.

FIGURE 4-6:
Frames
that aren't
selected
appear
dimmed.

Adding details

In the screen that displays your video (refer to Figure 4-4), tap Next. The New Post screen appears, as shown in Figure 4-7.

On this screen, you can add a caption, include a location where the video was recorded, add a fundraiser for a cause you support, share the video on other social media networks, and turn commenting on and off. The process for adding all this good stuff is described in Chapter 3.

Posting your video

When you're ready to post your video, tap Share at the bottom of the New Post screen on iOS devices, or the check mark in the upper-right corner on Android devices (refer to Figure 4-7). After a few seconds, your video appears on the Instagram home screen, as shown in Figure 4-8.

The video starts playing as soon as you view it and will play continuously every time you view the post. The video plays without sound, but you can turn on the sound by tapping the speaker icon in the lower-right corner of the video.

FIGURE 4-8:
The video
plays on the
home
screen.

Uploading a Stored Video

It's easy to upload a video that you've already recorded and stored on your iPhone, iPad, or Android smartphone or tablet. Simply follow these steps:

1. **Tap the plus (+) icon at the top of the Instagram feed screen.**

2. **Tap Post in the drop-down menu.**

3. **Select the video you want to upload by tapping its thumbnail image in the Recents section, as shown in Figure 4-9.**

   The video plays continuously in the viewer. Stop playback by tapping anywhere in the viewer.

Instagram automatically crops your video to the size of the viewer, but you can resize the video to its original size by tapping the resize icon (labeled in Figure 4-9).

4. **(Optional) Apply a filter, change the cover frame, and trim your video.**

These tasks are described in the "Improving Your Video" section, earlier in this chapter.

5. **Tap Next.**

6. **(Optional) Add a caption and a location, specify other social networks where you want to share your video, and turn commenting on or off.**

These tasks are the same for photos and videos. For details, see the section on enriching photos in Chapter 3.

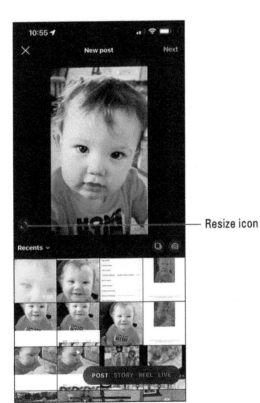

Resize icon

FIGURE 4-9: The selected video thumbnail image is faded so you know it's the video playing in the viewer.

Uploading Multiple Videos from an iPhone or iPad

If you've already taken videos with your iPhone or iPad and saved them to your Camera Roll, you can upload them to a single Instagram video and share it with your followers. Sorry, Android users; this feature isn't available on Android smartphones yet.

Follow these steps to upload multiple clips into one Instagram video:

1. Tap the plus (+) icon on the Instagram feed screen.

2. Tap Post in the drop-down menu.

3. Select the first video you want to upload by tapping its thumbnail image in the New Post screen.

4. Tap a second video you want to upload.

5. Tap Next.

    The Filter screen appears, and the viewer plays the first video. The second video appears to the right of the first video (see Figure 4-10). The video that's playing plays first in the video followed by the second video.

6. In the viewer, tap the video you want to edit.

7. Tap Trim, at the bottom of the screen.

    The Trim screen appears, and your selected video plays in the viewer.

8. Trim the first video.

    These tasks are described in the "Improving Your Video" section earlier in the chapter, with the exception that the resize bars in the timeline are black instead of white.

9. Tap Done.

    The Filter screen appears.

10. **Repeat Steps 5 through 9 for the second video.**

As you add each clip, Instagram assigns it a number indicating its order in the video.

WARNING

If you add a clip that puts your video over the 60-second limit, Instagram automatically trims the last clip so that your entire video lasts for exactly 60 seconds.

11. **Tap Next.**

The New Post screen appears.

12. **(Optional) Type a caption, add a location, share your video on other social networks, and turn commenting on or off.**

For more information, read the section on enriching photos in Chapter 3. All the information there applies not only to photos but also to videos.

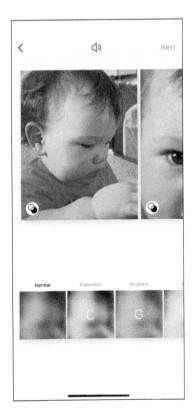

FIGURE 4-10:
Tap anywhere in the first video to pause playback.

REMEMBER

When you upload a video with multiple clips, you can't change the orientation of the clips to landscape or portrait. Each clip appears in its original orientation, so keep that in mind when you want to create a video with multiple clips.

Uploading Longer Videos via Desktop Web Browsers

Instagram allows you to upload videos of up to ten minutes in length via the Instagram website on a desktop web browser.

Follow these steps to upload videos on the Instagram website:

1. Log into Instagram.com with your Instagram account.

2. Click on the plus (+) icon in the upper-right corner of the screen.

3. Drag and drop your video file into the upload screen.

4. If you want to change the orientation of the video from the default square ratio, click the double arrow icon in the lower-left corner of the viewer and select the ratio to upload.

5. Click Next in the upper-right corner of the screen.

6. (Optional) Choose your cover image frame, trim the video, and manage the sound for the video.

7. Click Next in the upper-right corner of the screen.

8. In the editing screen, write your caption, add your location, and tag others as previously described in this chapter.

9. Click Share in the upper-right corner to post your video to Instagram.

REMEMBER

You can't edit or add filters to videos when you upload via the Instagram website.

3

Connecting with a Community on Instagram

Chapter **5**

Finding People to Follow

G rowing your Instagram following is one of the hottest topics on Instagram. If you've spent any time there, surely you've encountered sales pitches to buy followers or purchase a crazy software program to increase likes and follows. Don't do it. Yes, it's impressive having a big following, especially when starting your account. However, any followers you buy are likely fake accounts or people who would never interact with you.

In this chapter, you discover how to find followers the right way. First, you see how Instagram can access the contact list on your phone to find more followers. Next, you discover ways to explore and search for followers in the Instagram app. After you start getting followers, find out who is worth following back and when it's best not to bother. Finally, find out how to develop a tribe — an online family that helps and supports you along the way as you grow your account.

Finding Your Peeps

If you're new to Instagram, you may be wondering where to start. Instagram is happy to help you make connections. One way Instagram can help you connect with others is through the contacts stored on your phone or tablet. After you activate this feature, your contacts are periodically synced with Instagram's servers. Instagram does not follow anyone on your behalf, and you can disconnect your contacts at any time so that Instagram can't access them.

WARNING

For privacy purposes, this feature may be best as a one-and-done in the beginning versus a constant connection.

To connect your contacts, follow these steps:

1. **Go to your Instagram profile page by tapping your photo at the bottom right of your phone's screen.**

2. **Tap the three lines at the top right.**

3. **Tap Settings.**

   The next screen offers you a variety of account settings to choose from.

4. **Tap Account.**

5. **To proceed, scroll down and tap Contacts Syncing.**

   The next screen offers you the ability to have Instagram periodically sync and store your contacts on Instagram's servers. Instagram does not auto-follow them for you; you can pick which contacts to follow.

6. **Slide the tab at the top right so it turns blue to allow syncing.**

   You may also see a pop-up to confirm the sync. Accept the sync to proceed.

7. **Tap the back arrow at the top left of the screen twice to get back to the main Settings menu.**

8. **Tap Follow and Invite Friends and then select how you would like to invite friends: by SMS (text message), by email, by other options available on your phone, or by following Facebook friends.**

9. The first three options create a message to be sent to contacts with a link to connect to your account.

10. Following Facebook Friends takes you to a page where you can either Discover People or choose Facebook.

11. Tap Follow next to the names of the people you would like to follow, as shown in Figure 5-1.

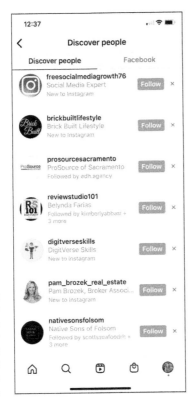

FIGURE 5-1: Instagram can suggest people for you to discover or show you Facebook friends to follow.

If you change your mind at some point and want to disallow Instagram's access to your contacts, tap the three lines on your profile page, tap Settings, tap Accounts, and then tap Contacts Syncing. Tap the Connect Contacts tab to return it to white, which terminates Instagram's access.

Some of your friends may have set their accounts to private. In this case, you see Requested after you tap Follow. They need to approve you before you can view their profile and posts.

Finding New Friends

Now that you've found your phone contacts on Instagram, it's time to follow the people who you may have a genuine interest in based on the content they provide. Instagram offers several options for exploring, searching, and suggesting new followers to you.

Exploring the Explore function

Instagram loves engagement. When people are actively engaging with others, it makes them more likely to stay on the platform rather than going somewhere else like TikTok or Twitter. And to keep those people, Instagram offers many ways to engage with them. One way is through the Explore page. The Explore page offers photo, video, and Reel posts that Instagram thinks may be interesting to you.

The Explore page is algorithmically sorted and selects content based on the likelihood that you'll like the content. The more you interact with certain types of content, the more of that you will see on the Explore page.

Here's how to use the Explore page:

1. **Tap the magnifying glass at the bottom of any screen.**

    Several photos, videos, and Reels are presented, as shown in Figure 5-2.

2. **Tap any post that interests you.**

    Now you can scroll down to see that post and other similar posts.

3. **Tap the Instagram username at the top of any post that interests you.**

4. **Look around the account. If you like what you see:**

- **Like one or more photos:** Double-tap each individual photo or tap the heart icon.

- **Leave a comment:** Tap the photo/video/Reel and then tap the comment bubble. Enter your text and tap the blue Post link.

- **To follow a user:** Tap the blue Follow button at the top of the user's profile page.

After you follow this page, Instagram offers several other accounts that it thinks you'd enjoy following. We detail this method of finding accounts to follow in the "Letting Instagram suggest users to you" section, later in this chapter.

FIGURE 5-2:
The Explore page displays a variety of posts you might like.

TIP

This method of finding followers is time consuming. Also, popular accounts may not be looking to follow many new people, so there's no guarantee that you'll get a reciprocal follow. However, it's always worth a shot and is a nice addition to your follower strategy.

Searching the Search feature

Another great way to find new accounts to follow is through searching Instagram. Instagram offers five ways to search: Top, Accounts, Audio, Tags, and Places.

To try out the Search feature, tap the magnifying glass on any page. The Explore page appears, as described in the preceding section. Tap the Search field at the top of the page, and enter a search word or phrase. Tap See All Results, and then you see Top, Accounts, Audio, Tags, and Places are now available for your choosing, as shown in Figure 5-3. (Android users see icons under the Search bar.)

The *Top* feature shows you accounts that match the general topic you typed in the search bar. To find new followers, search for a topic or a keyword that interests you. For instance, typing **healthy eating** presents several accounts that have content related to nutrition and healthy eating. Scroll through those that are interesting and follow those you like.

The *Accounts* feature can be used in a similar manner to the Top feature, but you may also choose to search by someone's name. If you have a list of names, try searching for people by name. For those that pop up, scroll through to their accounts and follow them if they seem to be active. Personal accounts are more likely to be private, so you'll need to request access.

The *Audio* feature presents audio that matches your search terms. Tap on the photo of the audio track to go to the page for that audio. You can save the audio to use on a Reel later, scroll through Reels by other people using that sound, or choose to use the audio and start a Reel using that sound immediately by tapping the Use Audio button that appears at the bottom of the screen.

FIGURE 5-3:
Search by
Top,
Accounts,
Audio, Tags,
and Places.

The *Tags* feature allows you to search by hashtag. Start simply by choosing your interest and see what appears. For example, if you're a dog trainer, start with #dogtraining, or even type just dog training without the hashtag symbol. If you get too many results to be useful, add your city or state, such as #dogtrain-ingsacramento. Scroll through the accounts and tap the ones that call out to you. Then follow the ones that seem active and engaging.

The *Places* feature enables you to search by location. Depending on what your search term is, the results present places that fit those search terms. If you allow your location services to be on, you can find people or businesses near you by tapping Near Current Location. Several nearby locations pop up for your choosing. Tap a location near you, and all the posts that marked that location on their post pop up. Tap some posts that catch your eye, and follow the ones you like.

On all the accounts you follow, make sure to like several posts and leave a meaningful comment or two (not just an emoji). This technique greatly increases the odds that the account will follow you back.

Letting Instagram suggest users to you

Instagram is on a mission to grow. Therefore, its main goal is making its users happy by making their accounts grow. When you follow someone, an algorithm kicks in and displays other similar accounts that you may like following. In Figure 5-4, we decide to follow @elevateitnow, a marketing and creative agency. Instagram then presents many other marketing business accounts, and we can decide whether to follow them.

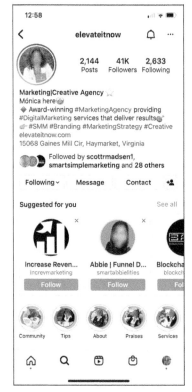

FIGURE 5-4:
After you follow an account, Instagram presents similar accounts you might like.

Deciding Who to Follow Back

After you've employed the techniques described previously in this chapter, you'll begin to get more followers. It's a great feeling to see that number go up on your profile page. Your next decision is whether to follow those accounts back if you weren't already following them. In this section, you discover how to view your followers and decide who is best to follow back.

Viewing and following your followers

So, you're starting to see more followers on your account. Now it's time to discover a simple method to follow them back. You're not required or even expected to follow someone back, but searching through your followers often yields some great finds! New followers appear in your notifications, but if you don't check your notifications often, it's worth checking out your follower list every few days to see who you may want to follow back.

Checking your follower list is easy:

1. **Go to your profile page and tap the number above** *followers.*

   All of your followers appear, with the most recent followers at the top. As shown in Figure 5-5, followers you haven't followed back have a blue Follow link to the right that you can tap to follow. If you're already following an account, there is a remove button.

2. **Unless you recognize the username, tap that name to view the user's profile page.**

3. **If you think that the user is someone you'd like to follow, tap the blue Follow button on their profile page. Otherwise, use the arrow on the top left of the page to go back to your follower list and try again.**

4. **Like a few posts and leave a meaningful comment.**

   When you like posts from an account, that follower is more likely to engage with you in the future.

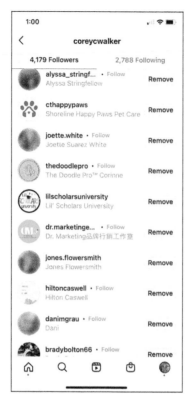

FIGURE 5-5:
Followers
you haven't
followed
back have a
blue Follow
link to the
right.

Reciprocating a follow or not

Now that you know a simple method for following back, the question is whether the account is worthy of following back. Some accounts have a habit of following accounts but then unfollowing them if they didn't follow back. You might see your numbers rise by 25, just to fall back by 22 the next day. It's a frustrating game that you should avoid.

Do follow back the following:

>> Accounts of friends, local businesses, and other people you know and like in real life (or as the kids say, "IRL")

>> Accounts of businesses you do business with or other related associates

>> Accounts that provide content inspiration

- Accounts of people you have met on other networks, such as Facebook, Twitter, or LinkedIn

- Accounts that you find personally interesting and satisfying to view and interact with

Don't follow back:

- Everyone who follows you because you feel some sort of obligation.

- Spammy accounts whose profiles probably list only a few posts and who often sell follower services.

- Accounts that use bots to leave automated comments. (Nothing is worse than having someone write "Love it!" when you post that your dog just died.)

- Accounts that contain content you have no interest in personally or professionally.

- Accounts that follow you for a few days, then unfollow you, and then follow you again a week later. They often use the #follow4follow hashtag, which means if you follow them, they will follow you back. Stay away!

TIP

You may discover your own rules for following accounts. Keep in mind that it's okay to unfollow people, too. Maybe they stopped posting, or their content no longer interests you. If you tap on your Following list from your profile, Instagram presents a category called Least Interacted With. Tap that to view those accounts. Tap the following button to unfollow an account. Clean up your feed every so often to ensure that you're viewing the best content for you.

Finding Your Squad

If you compare all the popular social networks — Facebook, Twitter, LinkedIn, and Instagram — the one that takes the cake on community engagement is Instagram. This section explains how to use hashtags, influencers, and interaction to find your ultimate Insta-squad!

If you've been on Instagram for a while, you've probably seen posts talking about community. But what does that mean? A *community* is a supportive group of people talking about and interacting with you on Instagram. They offer advice, give a heads-up about changes on Instagram, provide support, and leave comments that can help boost your posts.

Your first step is finding a community that fits with your interests. An easy way to do this is through hashtags. A hashtag link is formed when someone places the # sign before a word or phrase. That link goes to a separate page on Instagram displaying other content using that hashtag. It also displays other similar hashtags. If you like cats, for example, searching #cats yields several other relevant hashtags such as #catsofinstagram, #catstagram, #catscatscats, #catsagram, #catsoftheday, and #fluffycat.

Choose one hashtag to tap, and you see Top, Recent, and Reels (as shown in Figure 5-6). Tap to follow any of the accounts that interest you and share your mutual interest of whatever you like most by commenting and liking their posts.

While you're commenting on their posts, you'll probably start seeing other people showing up frequently on the same accounts. Follow, like, and comment on those accounts, too, and before you know it, your squad is developing!

To further solidify your relationship, send other account owners direct messages (DMs) to introduce yourself. (DMs are covered in Chapter 6.) Let the relationship flow naturally, and tell them how much you enjoy the conversations you've had.

You may also find your squad completely away from Instagram. For example, Facebook groups catering to niche markets often have Instagram communities that coincide with the group. They may have their own unique hashtags to easily identify them on Instagram. You may also discover them by following the admin of the group and seeing the same people interacting on Instagram.

Not finding the community you're seeking? Start your own! Run a contest or campaign asking people to submit a photo that goes with your hashtag. For example, if you're a graphic designer, you could start a challenge using #graphicdesignotd, where designers post what they worked on that day. People love challenges like this because it provides post inspiration and an excuse to show off their work! Keep checking the hashtag for submissions, and thank everyone for participating. Then follow them, and keep coming back regularly, commenting and liking their posts. All of a sudden, a squad is forming!

REMEMBER

With any of these methods for finding or creating your community, the most important element is engagement. By liking and commenting often, you get the same in return. Members get to know each other on a deeper level by watching for those special posts every day. Like the old saying goes: The more you give, the more you get back!

IN THIS CHAPTER

» Sending and responding to direct messages on Instagram

» Sharing photos, videos, and GIFs

» Recording and sending a voice message

» Messaging with a group

» Chatting live with other Instagram users

» Managing your inbox and deleting messages

Chapter **6**

Direct Messaging with Others

Posting photos and videos to your profile is just one of many ways to share your content. You can also use the Instagram Direct service to send a private message to a single follower or a group of 2 to 32 followers.

This chapter tells you all about how to share a direct message with your friends and fans. Because anyone can follow you (unless your account is private), direct messaging is Instagram's way of letting you connect with one person or a group of people in a private setting.

In this chapter, we start by showing you how to send a simple text message via Instagram Direct. Then we get more advanced with sending photos, videos, GIFs, music, and voice messages and show you how to reply to the direct messages you receive.

Next, you discover how to use the live chat feature within Instagram Direct. Finally, we show you how to navigate (delete and mute) through the messages you've sent and received so your inbox doesn't get overwhelmed with messages.

Starting a New Direct Message

If you want to start your conversation with a text message, Instagram makes it easy for you. Follow these steps:

1. **If the Direct screen isn't open, tap the Instagram Direct icon (it looks like a talking bubble with a squiggle) in the upper-right corner of your home screen (see Figure 6-1).**

   This is also where you receive new messages. The number of messages waiting for you is shown in a red circle on top of the Direct icon. Your new messages are revealed when you tap the number.

FIGURE 6-1: The Instagram Direct icon is located at the top right of your home screen.

2. Tap the pencil in a square icon as shown in Figure 6-2.

The New Message screen appears.

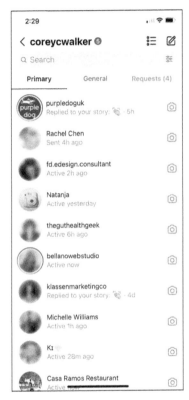

FIGURE 6-2:
Create a
new
message by
tapping the
pencil icon
at the upper
right of your
screen.

3. Search for a name in the Search box or scroll in the Suggested list to find the recipients, and then tap their usernames (see Figure 6-3).

A blue check mark appears to the right of each recipient name after you tap it.

4. On iPhone, tap Chat. On Android, the message box appears at the bottom of the screen after you select one or more recipients.

5. Start typing in the message box at the bottom of the page, and tap Send when you have completed your message (see Figure 6-4).

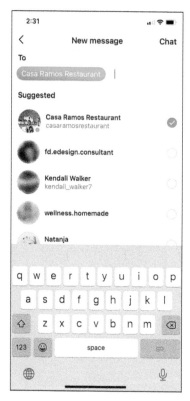

FIGURE 6-3:
The New
Message
page allows
you to select
message
recipients.

6. **Return to the Direct screen by tapping the < icon.**

   The message you just sent appears at the top of the list. Each message entry in the list shows you the recipient's or group's name, followed by whether the recipient is active now (by showing a green dot on their profile image) or when they were last active.

   View your message on the screen by tapping the message entry.

7. **Return to the Instagram home screen by tapping the < icon.**

TIP

You can unsend a message by holding down on the message. Then tap Unsend (iPhone) or Unsend Message (Android) to unsend it. The message has now been erased from the conversation (but it may have been seen if the contact is quick to read messages!).

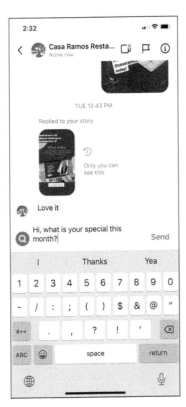

FIGURE 6-4:
Type a new message in the Message screen at the bottom of the page.

TIP

You can send messages without notifications to friends if it's late at night or when they're working by adding "@silent" in your message.

Sharing Photos and Videos via Direct Message

If sending a text message is too boring for you, you can take a photo or video (or use one from your camera roll) and send it to the other person. You can even customize the photo with text, filters, GIFs, and more.

1. **In the main Direct screen, tap the Camera icon to the right of the recipient as shown in Figure 6-5.**

If you need to get to the Direct screen, first tap the Direct icon from the Instagram home screen or window.

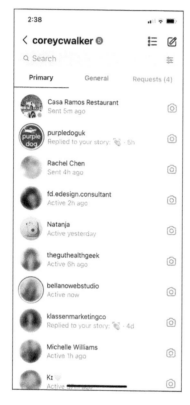

FIGURE 6-5:
The Camera icon is at the right of each recent recipient on the main Instagram Direct page.

2. **Take a photo by tapping the shutter button (as shown in Figure 6-6) or hold the white button down to film a video. Alternatively, you can choose a photo or video from your camera roll by tapping the small square at the lower left of the camera screen and choosing the photo/video by tapping it.**

   The switch cameras icon appears to the bottom right of the shutter button so you can switch between the front and rear cameras, if necessary. If you're unhappy with what you shot, tap the X to delete the photo or video and try again.

FIGURE 6-6:
Tap (for photos) or hold (for videos) the white button to take a photo or video.

3. **If you want to layer text on top of your photo or video, tap on the text (Aa) icon once you've chosen your photo (otherwise you'll be sent to the Create screen). Type your message (as shown in Figure 6-7), and then tap Done.**

Photos and videos here have all the same custom capabilities as they do in Instagram stories. For more information about how to add filters, GIFs, polls and more, refer to Chapter 8.

4. **After any customizing is complete, you can decide how you want the photo to be viewed by tapping Allow Replay, View Once, or Keep in Chat.**

View Once allows one view and then the photo or video disappears. *Allow Replay* allows one view and one replay, then the photo or video disappears. *Keep in Chat* keeps the photo or video in the message thread indefinitely.

FIGURE 6-7:
Add text to
your photo
by tapping
the Aa.

5. **Tap Send at the lower right.**

The photo is sent right away to the contact you chose.

TIP

You can search for a recipient by tapping the Search box above the list and typing your search terms. As you type, the usernames that most closely match your terms appear in the results list. When you find the name of the recipient you're looking for, tap their name in the list.

WARNING

Direct messages are private, and Instagram means it — you can't do several things with a direct message that you can do with a public message:

» You can't share photos or videos sent with Instagram Direct to other social networking websites.

» Any hashtags or locations you add to your private message aren't searchable in Instagram.

>> Your messages won't appear in the feed screen or in your profile.

TIP

If you want to send a photo or video you took previously, you can choose one from your camera roll by tapping the small square at the lower left of the camera screen and choosing the photo/video by tapping it, as shown in Figure 6-8. You can also choose multiple photos/videos at once by tapping Select, tapping each thumbnail you want, and tapping the arrow at the bottom of the screen.

FIGURE 6-8:
Choose from the photos or videos within your camera roll by tapping on them.

Sharing GIFs

Sometimes all you need to communicate a message is a fun GIF. Instagram imports hundreds of available GIFs via Giphy for you to use in Instagram Direct.

To send a GIF in a message, follow these steps:

1. **Tap or click the Instagram Direct icon.**

2. **Type in the Search feature (or scroll through your recent messages list) to locate the contact you want and tap their name then tap Chat to reveal the message screen.**

3. **Tap the black + button located in the right corner of the Message bar at the bottom of the screen as shown in Figure 6-9.**

   A Stickers button with a smiley face then appears.

4. **Tap the button to see suggested GIFs, as shown in Figure 6-10.**

   You can also use the Search Giphy bar to search for specific GIFs.

FIGURE 6-9:
Reveal the stickers button by tapping the black + button in the Message box.

FIGURE 6-10:
You can
select from
suggested
GIFs, or you
can search
for other
GIFs.

5. **Tap the GIF you like best.**

   It automatically sends the GIF, so be careful what you tap!

Using Voice Messages

Tired of typing, or have a lot to say, and prefer to leave a quick voice message? Instagram has a solution for that!

To send a voice message, follow these steps:

1. **Tap or click the Instagram Direct icon.**

2. **Type in the Search feature (or scroll through your recent messages list) to locate the contact you want and tap their name to reveal the message screen.**

3. **Press and hold the microphone icon located in the right corner of the Message bar (as shown in Figure 6-11) while recording a message of up to one minute.**

WARNING

When recording a voice message by tapping and holding, the message will automatically send when you release the microphone button. You can also tap the microphone, speak, then tap the arrow to send it. If you want to delete the message and rerecord it, tap the trash can on the left before sending it; then hold down the microphone again to rerecord.

FIGURE 6-11: Press and hold the microphone icon while recording your voice message.

Creating a New Group Message

If you'd like to send a private message to two or more people at once, you can create a group conversation. Use the following steps to create a new group conversation:

1. **Tap the Instagram Direct icon.**

2. **Tap the pencil icon at the upper right of the screen.**

3. **Type names in the Search feature (or scroll through the Suggested list) to locate the contacts you want and tap the circle to the right of their names.**

   The names appear in blue at the top of the screen and can be deleted by tapping their (now blue) names in the To field. Once the name turns red, tap it again to fully remove it from the group conversation.

4. **Tap Chat.**

   The next screen appears and allows you to enter a name for the group.

5. **Enter the name of the group, as shown in Figure 6-12.**

   This group is saved after you name it. You can send other messages to the same group later by looking for it in the Search box or scrolling through your sent messages.

TIP

   You can rename your group later by tapping the group name and entering a new name. The members of the group are able to see this name, so choose wisely!

6. **Type a message, take a photo or video, or send a GIF or a voice message to the group.**

   Instructions for sending each of these message types are outlined earlier in the chapter and are the same for single and group messages.

If you need to include more group members later, there's an easy way to do that. Simply tap the group name, tap Add People, search and select the contacts you'd like to add, and tap Next (iPhone) or Done (Android). The new group members are now added to your thread and can see the entire previous conversation except for any disappearing photos or videos.

Replying to a Direct Message

If you've had a previous conversation with one or more recipients, you can tap the individual or group name in the Direct screen to view your past conversation(s) and write a new message to start a new conversation. The Message screen appears, and you see all the text, photos, and videos you sent previously to that recipient or that group.

Swipe or scroll to view your entire conversation. You can also type a new message, as described earlier in this chapter.

If you're already having a private message conversation in Instagram Direct, you can respond by sending a photo to one or more of your follower as described earlier in the "Sharing Photos and Videos via Direct Message."

Using Live Chat in Direct Messages

Sometimes it's nice to carry on a conversation face-to-face, even if it's not in person. You can now live chat with up to six people using Instagram Direct.

To use video chat on Instagram:

1. **Tap the Instagram Direct icon.**

2. **Type in the Search feature (or scroll through your recent messages list) to locate the contact or group you want and tap their name to reveal the message screen.**

3. **Tap the movie camera icon at the top right of the screen, as shown in Figure 6-13.**

FIGURE 6-13: Live Chat is accessed by tapping the movie camera icon at the top of the message screen.

The contact or group is notified that you're requesting a live chat and can choose to answer or dismiss the call as shown in Figure 6-14.

FIGURE 6-14:
Your contact
is notified
that you'd
like to live
chat.

WARNING

Anyone you've direct messaged with previously can request a live chat. If you don't want them to have this capability, on iPhone you can Mute Video Chat by scrolling to their name, swiping left, and then tapping More; then tap Mute, then Mute Video Chat. On Android, you hold down on the person's name and choose Mute Video Chats from the pop-up list of options.

If you've already started a chat with one or more people, you can add more people (up to six people total on the chat) to an ongoing conversation.

To add more people to your video chat, follow these steps:

1. **While still in your video chat, simply swipe up to add another contact.**

    Your list of recently messaged contacts is shown. You can use Search to find other contacts.

2. **When you've located your contact, tap Add next to their user name.**

    The contact receives a notification that you'd like to video chat, and they can pick up the chat, ignore it, or choose to decline it.

Quick Sharing Content with Friends

See something interesting in your feed that you'd like to share with a friend? You can now quickly share the post with a friend by doing the following:

1. **Tap and hold the paper airplane arrow below the content in your feed that you'd like to share (see Figure 6-15).**

2. **Slide up on the profile icon of the person you'd like to send the content to.**

That piece of content shoots off right away to the recipient, so watch your fingers!

FIGURE 6-15:
Share
content with
friends by
tapping and
holding the
paper
airplane
icon.

Navigating Your Inbox

If you've been following the instructions within this chapter, you likely have several message threads piling up in your Instagram Direct inbox that you need to manage. You may have even discovered some contacts you'd rather not hear from anymore.

New messages are indicated by a red circle with the number of messages on top of the Direct icon located at the top of your home screen, as shown in Figure 6-16. By tapping the Direct icon, you are taken to the Messages screen where you can tap on the new message to view it.

When you're done viewing the message, you have choices to make:

FIGURE 6-16:
You are
notified
about new
direct
messages by
a red circle
with the
number of
messages
on top of
the
Instagram
Direct icon
on the home
screen.

» Let it sit in your inbox indefinitely.

» Reply to the message with text, a photo, a video, a GIF, or a heart (as described earlier).

» Delete the message. On an iPhone, swipe left and tap Delete. On Android, hold down over the account name and choose Delete from the pop-up menu. (See Figure 6-17.)

» Mute the conversation so they can no longer contact you on Instagram Direct. Swipe left and tap More; then tap Mute. (See Figure 6-18.)

» Flag the message to remember to view it later. On iPhones, swipe left, tap More, and tap Flag. On Android, tap and hold on the message and select Flag from the pop-up menu.

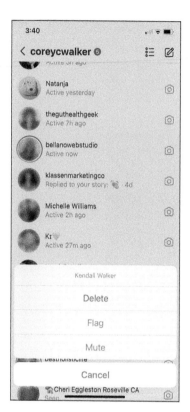

FIGURE 6-17:
Deleting a
message.

» Mark the message as Unread so it's highlighted in bold again. On iPhones, swipe left and tap Unread. On Android, tap and hold on the message and select "Mark as Unread" from the pop-up menu.

That's really all there is to it! The Instagram Direct inbox is fairly simple to navigate with limited options for handling your messages after viewing them.

Instagram Direct's message search capabilities are slim. At this point, you can only search for messages based on the contact or group's name. Unlike an email inbox, you can't filter a search by subject, keywords, or date.

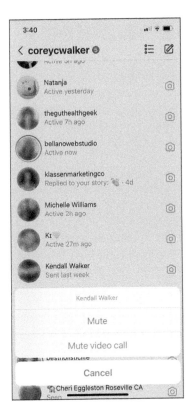

FIGURE 6-18:
Muting a
conversation.

To search for a conversation by username or group name, follow these steps:

1. **Tap the Instagram Direct icon.**

2. **Type in the Search feature (or scroll through your recent messages list) to locate the contact or group you want and tap their name.**

   Once the name is tapped, you see your previous conversation and can choose to reply if you'd like.

Getting Rid of Unwanted Messages

Instagram is a huge platform with millions of users. This can result in messages from a variety of sources, and there's a good chance you'll receive a message from someone that you'd rather not hear from.

If the user isn't someone you're following or you've messaged previously, Instagram funnels them into a different section. You see their initial request to speak with you with a blue Requests link that indicates the number of requests waiting. When you tap that blue link, a new page appears, revealing the usernames of the people who would like to contact you. You now have choices to make (as shown in Figure 6-19):

» Swipe left and tap Accept to allow communication between you, Block to deny any further contact, or Delete to delete the message.

» If several messages are waiting from users you don't want to communicate with, Instagram makes it easy with a Delete all link at the bottom. Tap that link to decline any future messages from those usernames.

You may have started a conversation with someone only to find out later that they're sending inappropriate messages. If you feel they should be reported for their actions, it's simple to do. To report an inappropriate message, follow these steps:

1. **Inside the conversation thread, tap and hold the individual comment that was inappropriate.**

   A Report button appears at the bottom of the page.

2. **Tap the Report button and follow the instructions.**

   The message and username is sent to Instagram and the user is reported. The user is not notified that you're the person who reported them.

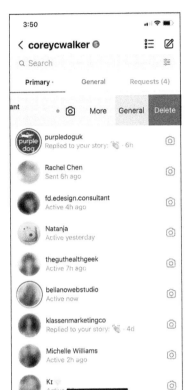

FIGURE 6-19:
A page
showing
your
message
requests
appears and
lets you
choose
whether to
allow them
to message
you, block
them
permanently,
or delete
their
messages.

Within the image:

3:50

< coreycwalker

Q Search

Primary ·   General   Requests (4)

ant   ⊙   More   General   Delete

purpledoguk
Replied to your story: 🎯 · 6h

Rachel Chen
Sent 6h ago

fd.edesign.consultant
Active 4h ago

Natanja
Active yesterday

theguthealthgeek
Active 7h ago

bellanowebstudio
Active now

klassenmarketingco
Replied to your story: 🎯 · 4d

Michelle Williams
Active 2h ago

Kı
Active

4

Telling Tales with Instagram Stories

Plan a story from beginning to end.

Experiment with different tools to personalize your stories.

Determine how to share stories in different ways.

Use Story Highlights to keep your stories forever.

Discover the excitement in going live on Instagram.

Chapter **7**

Creating Instagram Stories

In this chapter, we explain the history of Instagram stories, where to watch them, how to watch them, and their specifications for images and videos. We also go into more detail about how you can plan out the stories you share (if you intend on planning); deciding what to share; and exactly how to upload photos, videos, and images to your stories. We also discuss camera effects and how to save and access your stories after you've archived them.

Finding Stories to Watch

Stories are meant to be quick little windows into your day. They can be original photos or videos or can be posts or Reels shared from another user's account. Stories expire within 24 hours, so most users don't put hours of time designing them or creating the perfect video for them.

Instagram stories are located in a bar at the top of your newsfeed and are represented by a multicolored ring around the profile picture of the story's creator, as shown in Figure 7-1. Tap the profile picture, and the story opens full-screen for you to watch.

FIGURE 7-1: View stories by tapping a profile picture at the top of your newsfeed.

New stories (personalized for you based on who you follow) are shown first. By scrolling to the left, you can see all stories that the people you follow have published in the last 24 hours. The story vanishes 24 hours after it was posted.

When you view a person's story, they can see that you've watched it, as shown in Figure 7-2. There is currently no way to block this feature. So, be aware if you're looking at a story from an ex–significant other. They know!

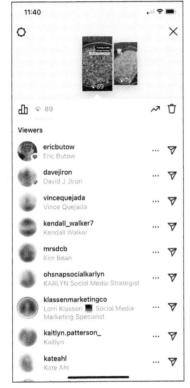

FIGURE 7-2:
You can see who saw your story by tapping on the Activity link at the bottom left of the screen or swiping up on your story.

Instagram stories are also accessible from the top left of a person's profile page. If the person has an active story, their profile picture has a multicolored ring around it, as shown in Figure 7-3. You don't need to be following the person to see their stories, as long as the account isn't private. Tap the profile picture, and the story opens full-screen for you to watch. After that person's stories have finished, the stories page closes and you're returned to their profile page.

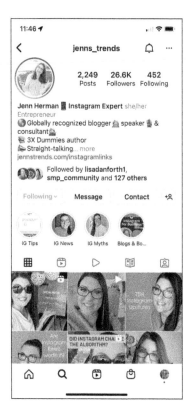

FIGURE 7-3:
View stories from a person's profile page by tapping their profile picture.

If you want to watch a continuing sequence of stories from people you follow, you must access the stories from the top of your Home feed. Instagram always takes you to the content you haven't seen in that person's story. For instance, if you'd watched two out of five stories by someone, Instagram would play the third story in the sequence when you came back within the 24-hour window of the post. Each person's story has white dashes at the top that indicate the number of stories for that person that day. Stories continue to play through each person's entire sequence and then go directly to the next person you're following who has a current story until you tap the X to exit (iPhone, as shown in Figure 7-4) or swipe down (Android) from Instagram stories.

FIGURE 7-4:
On iPhone,
tap the X at
the top right
of a story to
exit. On
Android,
swipe down.

Interacting with Stories You Watch

The next few sections describe how to interact with the stories you watch. You can find out how to skip the stories you're not interested in, how to rewatch things you want to see again, how to pause a story, and how to react to a story.

Forwarding through the things you don't like

To forward through one story within a person's full story sequence, simply tap on the right side of the screen. You'll skip to that person's next story, unless it's their last or only story; in that case, you'll be taken to the next person's story.

To forward through a person's entire sequence of stories, swipe left from the right side of the screen. You'll skip that person's full set of stories and move on to the next person's stories.

When you're finished watching, tap the X at the top right of the screen or swipe down to be returned to your Home screen.

Going back to the things you want to see again

To go back to the last story in the sequence you just watched, tap the left side of the screen to jump back to the previous post. Keep tapping if you want to keep going back.

To go back to a different person's sequence of stories, swipe right from the left side of the screen until you get back to that person's stories.

Similar to forwarding, if you're seeking a certain person's story, it's easier to go directly to their profile to watch or scroll through the circles at the top of your Home screen to find that person.

When you're finished watching, tap the X at the top right of the screen or swipe down to be returned to your Home screen.

Pausing a story to see more

Stories tend to whip by pretty fast, and sometimes people add lots of text or talk really fast to squeeze a lot of info in. Lucky for you, there is a way to pause a story so you can take it all in. To pause a story, just tap and hold anywhere on the screen, and the story remains frozen until you let go.

Reacting to a story

Reactions to stories now include likes, reactions, or direct messages.

To like a story, simply tap the heart on the bottom right of the screen. The story creator will be notified.

To send a direct message in response to a story, follow these steps:

1. **Tap the Send Message area at the bottom of the screen.**

   Quick Reactions (emojis) and a keyboard appear, as shown in Figure 7-5.

2. **Type a message, select a GIF, or use one of the Quick Reaction emojis above the keyboard.**

3. **When your message is complete, tap Send to send your message.**

FIGURE 7-5:
Send a
message by
tapping in
the Send
Message
box, typing a
message,
and tapping
Send.

Understanding story limitations

If you've watched a few Instagram Stories, you've probably noticed that they're all in vertical or portrait mode, and videos are in short sequences. Videos and photos in stories work best if they are in the following formats:

>> **Image ratio:** 4:5 (vertical only) or 9:16 for photos

>> **Image size minimum:** 600-x-1,067 pixels

>> **Image size maximum:** 1,080-x-1,920 pixels

>> **File type:** PNG or JPG for photos/graphics; MP4 or MOV for videos

>> **File size max:** 30MB for photos; 4GB for videos

Accessing the Story Camera

Accessing the story camera is easy but not always obvious. There are a few methods for accessing the camera:

>> From the Home page, swipe right.

>> From the Home page, tap the + sign at the top right of the screen; then tap Story.

>> If you do not have any stories running currently, tap your profile picture on the Home page or your personal profile. If there is a blue plus (+) sign next to your profile picture, you'll be able to access the camera to create a new story.

When you're on the story creation page, the camera is available for taking photos or videos via the white button. Tap for photos; hold for videos for up to one minute. We provide details on what to share and how to add bells and whistles to your photos or videos in the next sections. *Note:* If you record a video longer than 15 seconds (up to one minute), it will be cut into individual video segments of 15 seconds when you upload it.

Planning a Story from Start to Finish

If you're using Instagram stories strictly for personal use, you may prefer to publish things on the fly as they happen rather than planning them. However, many businesses, brands, and influencers use stories in a much more strategic way to truly, well, tell a story.

TIP

If you want your followers to stand up and take notice of your stories, here are some planning tips to make them "next level":

>> Use a planning tool such as Later or Planoly to "lay out" and schedule your stories so you can view them as you would a storyboard. You can find these tools in the app store for your device or find them online on your desktop if you like to load graphics and videos from your computer.

>> Use consistent colors and fonts throughout the story so your story looks cohesive.

>> Use a template to make your stories easily identifiable as coming from you.

>> Think about which mentions or locations you want to add to your story.

Deciding What to Share

Instagram stories were designed to be a looser, less perfect part of Instagram. Many Instagrammers agonize over choosing the right photo or caption for their profile page so their aesthetic is flawless. Instagram stories allow those users to offer a less polished version of themselves and a glimpse into their everyday lives that automatically goes away in 24 hours. In this section, we detail some of the common ways people use Instagram stories.

Sharing your less-than-perfect stuff

You may want to share

>> **Behind the scenes photos and videos:** Because many Instagrammers are involved in launches, events, conferences, podcasts, and other exciting activities, behind-the-scenes stories are a great way to let your audience in on how the magic really happens. Whether it's showing the types of equipment used hanging decorations for an exclusive party, or interviewing speakers backstage before a conference starts, followers love to get to know more about you through behind-the-scenes stories.

>> **Travel photos:** You may have that one gorgeous, meticulously edited shot of your trip for your profile page, but you have *so* many more that you're dying to share right away! Stories are the perfect opportunity to load lots of photos that may not make the cut on your profile (like that funny one of your cousin wiping out on a boogie board).

Showcasing your personality and lifestyle

To showcase who you really are, you consider trying the following:

>> **Talking to the camera:** The popularity of video has surged in the last several years, so what better way to grab your followers' attention than by talking to them via Instagram stories (see Figure 7-6)? Talking directly to your followers gives them a familiarity with you that can't be matched through still images.

>> **Candid shots or videos:** Kids doing something silly around the house? Dog looking adorable (see Figure 7-7)? These are perfect moments to share with your followers in a story to show the day-to-day happenings around you.

FIGURE 7-6:
@wellness.
homemade
talks directly
to her
followers
regularly
using
stories.

FIGURE 7-7:
@vinceque-
jada shares
stories
about his
puppy.

>> **Before-and-after images and series:** Before-and-after shots and photo series are an exceptional way to tell a story. Maybe you recently remodeled your kitchen and want to show the differences, or you want to show the progression of a project that took you weeks to complete. Stories are a unique way to display the results along with how far you've come (see Figure 7-8).

FIGURE 7-8: @eggle-stondesigns shows videos about home staging using before-and-after stories.

Adding a Story Photo

To get started creating a photo story, follow these steps:

1. **From your newsfeed (home screen), swipe right or tap the + sign; then tap Story at the top right of the screen.**

You can also tap your profile picture with the blue plus sign in the row of stories at the top of your screen.

Make sure the setting at the bottom of the screen is Story, as shown in Figure 7-9.

FIGURE 7-9:
Tap the white circle in Story mode to take a basic photo with the stories camera.

2. **Take a photo.**

To take a photo, hold the phone vertically and tap the white circle.

If you want the phone in selfie mode (camera facing you versus away from you), tap the two arrows located to the bottom right of the white circle before you tap the white circle. You can also double tap anywhere on the screen to switch the camera back and forth between the front- and rear-facing cameras.

3. **To retake the photo or video, tap the X at the top left of the screen, and repeat Step 2.**

4. **Share your Story by tapping Your Story at the bottom left of the screen; send it to Close Friends only by tapping Close Friends to the right of the Your Story button; or send it as a DM by tapping the arrow at the bottom right of the screen, selecting Message, selecting the recipients, and tapping Send.**

A face filter is an app that applies a filter over your face using the camera, making you look, for example, like a dog, a rock star, or just bathed in a warm glow. Here's how to take a photo with a face filter:

1. **Open Instagram stories by swiping right or using the + sign at the top of the newsfeed.**

2. **Put the camera in selfie mode by tapping the arrows to the bottom right of the white circle.**

   Some filters can be used in rear-facing mode to add a filter, color, or lighting element.

3. **Scroll to the left or right of the white circle to see different filters.**

   If you scroll all the way to the left, you can search other filters. Instagram often adds new filters seasonally or when there are big events like the Super Bowl or the Grammys.

4. **To apply a filter, scroll the filter you want to use over the white button and it will show you what you'll look like using that filter as shown in Figure 7-10.**

   To change filters, simply scroll to the next one.

5. **Take a photo by tapping the white button or record a video by holding down the white button.**

6. **To try again, tap the X at the top left of the screen and go back to Step 4.** If you want to try the photo without a filter, simply scroll back so the button is white again.

7. **Share your story by tapping Your Story at the bottom left of the screen; send it to Close Friends only by tapping Close Friends; or send it as a DM by tapping the arrow, selecting Message, selecting the recipients, and tapping Send.**

FIGURE 7-10:
Face filters
allow you to
take on a
whole new
persona in
your story!

You may prefer to upload a photo stored on your camera roll instead of capturing it in the Instagram app.

TIP

When you swipe up or tap the small photo icon to load a photo or video, you see photos from the last 24 hours first. If you keep scrolling up, you'll see your entire camera roll, and you can load older items by tapping them.

Follow these steps to upload an existing photo to your story:

1. **Swipe right from the newsfeed or tap the + sign at the top right of the newsfeed, and tap Story to access your Instagram story.**

2. **Swipe up from the bottom of the screen or tap the box with a small photo thumbnail at the bottom left.**

   Thumbnails of all available photos and videos are displayed at the bottom of the screen, as shown in Figure 7-11.

3. **Tap the photo you'd like to post, or tap Select to choose up to ten photos.**

   Be sure to select them in the order you'd like them to appear in your story.

4. **To add a photo filter (not a face filter) to your photo, swipe right until you reach the filter option you want.**

5. **Share your story by tapping Your Story; send it to Close Friends only by tapping Close Friends; or send it as a DM by tapping the arrow, selecting Message, selecting the recipients, and tapping Send.**

FIGURE 7-11:
Swipe up from the bottom of the Instagram stories screen to see available photos to post.

Adding a Story Video

Video can definitely enhance your story, and it's always fun to include. A standard story video is only 15 seconds long, but in this section, we show you how to film up to a minute in length.

Filming with the stories camera

Filming a video within stories is very similar to taking a photo within stories. The main difference is holding down the button for video versus tapping it for a photo. Here are complete instructions for filming a video within stories:

1. **Swipe right from the newsfeed or tap the + sign at the top right of the newsfeed, and tap Story to access your Instagram story.**

   You can also tap your profile picture with the blue plus sign in the row of stories at the top of your screen.

   Make sure the setting at the bottom of the screen is on Story, as shown earlier in this chapter (refer to Figure 7-9).

2. **Take a video.**

   To take a video, hold the phone vertically and hold the white circle. On the iPhone, you see a red line form around the circle that lets you know how much time you have left within your available 60 seconds. On Android, you see a purple line that shifts to orange and yellow.

   If you want the phone in selfie mode (with the camera facing you instead of away from you), tap the two arrows located to the bottom right of the white circle before you tap the white circle.

   The camera saves the first 15 seconds in a thumbnail that shows directly above the white circle. It may allow you to film more than 1 minute, but it only allows you to *post* the four 15-second segments to total 1 minute.

3. **When you're done filming, release the white circle.**

   The video thumbnails move down to the lower left of the screen, as shown in Figure 7-12.

FIGURE 7-12:
Each
15-second
segment will
move down
to the
bottom left
of the
screen.

4. **To upload all segments of the video, tap the arrow at the bottom right of the screen.**

   You can then choose to share it to Your Story, share it with Close Friends, or DM someone.

5. **To retake the video, tap the X at the upper left of the screen, and repeat Step 2.**

6. **Share your story by tapping Your Story; send it to Close Friends only by tapping Close Friends; or send it as a DM by tapping the arrow, selecting Message, selecting the recipients, and tapping Send.**

You can also share videos from your camera roll to your story. Follow the instructions for uploading a photo from your camera roll detailed in the previous section.

TIP

Experimenting with all the camera options

Instagram stories pack a lot into their little piece of the Insta-world. Their camera has many added features to add fun and drama to your stories. In this section, we offer an overview of the different camera options.

Using Create

Create is already loaded automatically within stories and allows you to type a message in text or use some of the other fun features like those shown in Figure 7-13.

FIGURE 7-13:
The Create feature has many settings to choose from.

Follow these steps to use Create for a story:

1. Swipe right from the newsfeed or tap the + sign at the top right of the newsfeed, and tap Story to access your Instagram story. If your camera roll is showing, tap the camera to get to the stories screen.

2. Tap the Aa on the left of the screen to reveal the Create features.

3. Slide through the eight available features: Text, Shoutouts, Gifs, Templates, On This Day, Questions, Countdown, or Quiz.

4. Follow the prompts for the features you choose.

5. If you're not satisfied with your Story and you want to try again, tap the back arrow at the upper left and tap Discard to start over.

6. Share your story by tapping Your Story; send it to Close Friends only by tapping Close Friends; or send it as a DM by tapping the arrow, selecting Message, selecting the recipients, and tapping Send.

Tip: Refer to the next chapter to see more fun ways to add GIFs, stickers, and more to your story.

Using Boomerang for fun

Boomerang is a feature that takes a burst of photos and creates a looping backward and forward video clip from them. An action such as twirling a pencil or blowing a bubble becomes more exciting when played in a loop.

Follow these steps to use Boomerang:

1. Swipe right from the newsfeed or tap the + sign at the top right of the newsfeed, and tap Story to access your Instagram story. If your camera roll is showing, tap the camera to get to the stories screen.

2. Tap the Boomerang icon (infinity symbol) on the left side of the screen.

3. To switch from forward-facing video mode to selfie video mode and back, tap the arrows at the bottom right of the screen.

You can also use Boomerang with one of the face filters, as described in the earlier section "Adding a Story Photo."

4. **Tap the white circle with the Boomerang logo as shown in Figure 7-14.**

   You don't need to hold down the white button as you would for video. The app is actually taking several pictures in a rapid burst.

5. **If you're not satisfied with your Boomerang and you want to try again, tap the back arrow at the upper left and tap Discard, starting over at Step 4.**

6. **Share the Boomerang story by tapping Your Story; send it to Close Friends only by tapping Close Friends; or send it as a DM by tapping the arrow, selecting Message, selecting the recipients, and tapping Send.**

FIGURE 7-14: Tap the Boomerang symbol to let the app take rapid burst photos.

Using Layout to make a collage

The Layout feature lets you choose from several grid options to upload more than one photo for a story. Here's how to create a Layout story:

1. Swipe right from the newsfeed or tap the + sign at the top right of the newsfeed, and tap Story to access your Instagram story. If your camera roll is showing, tap the camera to get to the stories screen.

2. Tap the Layout icon (square with a rectangle with two small squares inside) on the left side of the screen.

3. Tap below the Layout icon to see other available layouts, and choose the one you like.

4. Take a photo for each section of your layout to fill in the grid as shown in Figure 7-15.

FIGURE 7-15:
Take photos
to fill each
section of
your layout.

5. If you're not satisfied with your Layout and you want to try again, tap X at the upper left and repeat, starting at Step 4.

6. Tap the check mark if you like the Layout and want to share it.

7. Share your story by tapping Your Story; send it to Close Friends only by tapping Close Friends; or send it as a DM by tapping the arrow, selecting Message, selecting the recipients, and tapping Send.

Using Hands-Free to make life easier

To film a video without the hassle of holding down the button the entire time, use the Hands-Free setting (the circle icon with a square inside of it) located on the left side of your story screen. You may need to tap the arrow on the left side of the screen to reveal the icon if it's not showing for you already. Once you tap the Hands-Free icon, you can record a video by tapping the white circle with the colorful circle inside. Tap the circle again to stop. If you don't tap it again, Hands-Free will keep filming a longer video, but it will only allow four 15-second segments to post as a "stitched together" video.

Saving Your Story

Sometimes stories are so good, you can't bear the thought of them disappearing forever. Well, you're in luck. You can save them to enjoy later and to repost on other social media networks in the following three ways.

Saving before publishing

After you create or upload a photo or video, tap the three dots at the top right of the screen (iPhone) bottom right of the screen (Android); then tap Save, and Instagram will save your photo or video to your camera roll (see Figure 7-16). You must do this before you tap Your Story or Close Friends.

FIGURE 7-16:
Tap the
three dots at
the top of
your screen
(on iPhone)
or bottom of
screen (on
Android)
and then tap
Save to save
your story.

| Delete |
| Save... |
| Share as post... |
| Send to... |
| Add Mentions |
| Copy link |
| Share to... |
| Add paid partnership label |
| Story settings |
| Cancel |

Saving after publishing

To save a story after you've published it but within its 24-hour window of being active, go to the newsfeed or your profile page and tap your profile picture. If you have an active story, it appears. Tap the right side of the screen until you see the story you want to save. Tap the three small dots at the lower right of the screen, and then tap Save (see Figure 7-17).

Automatically saving all your stories

Tap the gear icon (Settings) at the top right of the Add to my stories page. Tap Story, and then you can choose to Save to Camera Roll (saving all stories to your phone) or Save to Archive (saving all stories to an accessible archive on Instagram). You can also choose neither of these options (and your stories will not be saved anywhere), one or the other, or both! Sliding the slider to blue means that functionality is on. After you've made your selections, tap the arrow to exit the page, and then tap Done on the next page to get back to the story screen.

Accessing your archives

In the preceding section, we explain how to save your stories to Instagram's archives (saving precious space on your camera roll). Here, we show you how to access them.

From your Profile page, tap the three lines at the upper right of the screen and then tap Archive. All the stories that you've posted since enabling the archive are available for you to view or reshare (see Figure 7-18). Instagram also suggests memories of photos taken on that day in years past to view, and allows searching by date or location.

FIGURE 7-18:
Old stories
are available
for you to
view and
reshare.

Chapter **8**

Adding Style to Your Stories

I n this chapter, we explain how to take your Stories to another level by adding personalized style and content, including various stickers, animations, captions, doodles, and text. These features can be combined in a variety of ways to create your own unique style and message.

Jazzing Up Your Story Post Using Stickers

There are many fun stickers to choose from on Instagram. And they keep adding more, so there are always fun new ways to augment your content. In this section, we look at some of the more common stickers available and explain how you can use them in your content.

Stickers are available by tapping the sticker icon (the square smiley face icon at the top of the story screen; see the left image in Figure 8-1) after you've uploaded or taken a photo or video. Tapping the sticker icon opens a screen (or tray) with various options of stickers and emojis (see the right image in Figure 8-1).

FIGURE 8-1: Access story stickers by tapping the sticker icon that looks like a smiley face.

Location and mention stickers add more context

As discussed in Chapter 3, you can tag a location on an Instagram post, @mention someone, or use hashtags to search, you can do much the same with your Instagram stories.

Location stickers

Adding a location sticker to your post lets your followers know where you are. Including a tappable sticker in your story enables your viewers to see other posts about that location and find out more about it.

Tap the smiley face icon and then tap the Location sticker. You see a new screen with a list of nearby locations. You can scroll through this list and tap to select the location you want to add. If your location isn't listed or the location isn't near you when you're adding the story, you can type in the search bar for the name of the location you want to tag. You see a list of related locations, and you can select the correct one by tapping it (see Figure 8-2).

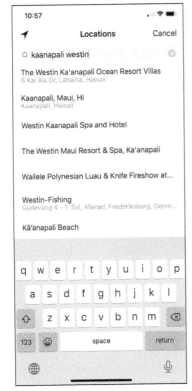

FIGURE 8-2:
Select your location from the list of locations or use the search bar to find the location of your choice.

After you select the location, the sticker appears on your story. You can pinch to zoom to make it smaller or larger. You can drag it around the screen or turn it on an angle to place it where you want.

You can also tap the location sticker to change the background of the sticker. There are typically three color options available that you can tap through (see Figure 8-3).

FIGURE 8-3:
Tap the location sticker to change its color or background.

Mention stickers

If you want to tag someone in your Instagram story, you simply have to tap the @Mention sticker on the sticker selection page.

First, find the person you want to mention by typing their name or username. Relevant users who match that name appear above the keyboard (see Figure 8-4). Keep typing until you find the person you're looking for; then tap their profile photo to select their username and add the sticker to your story. As with Location stickers, you can drag the sticker around, pinch to enlarge or shrink, and tap to change the background and color options.

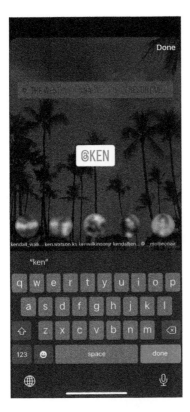

You can mention multiple people in your story. Simply add another @Mention sticker for each person you want to tag.

TIP

The person or people who are tagged in your story are notified via a direct message that you tagged them. They'll be able to see your story, and they'll be able to share your Story to their own Story.

REMEMBER

Add Yours, GIFs, sliders, emojis, and more

The previous two stickers are incredibly functional and help with search and exposure. But they don't do much for the fun factor or to drive engagement. Fortunately, there are plenty of other sticker options to up the fun factor!

Add Yours

The Add Yours sticker groups together a collection of stories on a theme (see Figure 8-5). You can add the Add Yours sticker to prompt your friends to add their own stories that are relevant to that theme. You can interact with an already existing sticker or start your own chain with a new Add Yours sticker. Common ideas include sharing vacation photos, highlighting your best friend (furry friends included), jumping on a popular trend, or starting a new challenge.

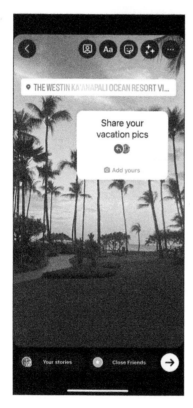

FIGURE 8-5:
The Add Yours sticker encourages friends to share a story based on your prompt.

GIF stickers

A cultural norm with social media is the use of GIFs (short, animated pieces) to convey a thought, emotion, or response. Instagram is partnered with Giphy so that you can add GIFs to your stories, too.

Select the GIF sticker option from the sticker screen. You can choose from a list of popular and trending GIFs. You can also search for a keyword or topic related to the GIF you want to use (see Figure 8-6).

FIGURE 8-6:
Use the search bar in the GIF sticker screen to find animations related to any topic of your choice.

You can add multiple GIFs to a story post to add the style and context you want. This is also a creative way to take a simple photo and make it animated and engaging.

Slider stickers

The Slider sticker is designed to boost engagement and interaction with your story. Viewers can physically drag the slider on the sticker to indicate their level of participation. You can find plenty of creative ways to utilize this sticker!

To add the sticker, select the Slider sticker (with the heart eyes emoji) from the sticker screen. Then select the emoji to include as the slider mechanism. Scroll left and right on the emojis to see all the available options. Then type in your question and tap Done when complete. You can drag and resize the sticker to place it anywhere on the image (see Figure 8-7).

FIGURE 8-7:
In this example, dragging the smiley face indicates how much people love seahorses.

Emojis

You have the whole emoji keyboard to utilize and add as stickers to your stories. Tap the sticker icon as shown in Figure 8-1 and scroll up on the sticker screen to reveal trendy stickers, emojis, and more.

Avatars

In the beginning of 2022, Instagram introduced Avatars. Once you have created your Avatar, you can add it as a sticker on Stories. An avatar, which is an animated character that is created in your likeness, is added to a number of stickers as shown in Figure 8-8.

FIGURE 8-8: Choose one of your personalized Avatar stickers to add to your story.

Questions, polls, quizzes, chats, and more

Do you want to find out more about your followers? Or maybe share more about yourself? The variety of questions, polls, quizzes, and chat stickers enable you to do that and encourage participation from your followers.

Questions sticker

The Questions sticker allows you to pose a question to your audience and have them submit responses. Your question can be on any topic you choose! Responses will appear in the story insights for that post and are only visible to you.

Select the Questions sticker from the sticker screen, type in a question and post the sticker to the story. Your followers have the option to type a response in the sticker itself. You can see the responses by tapping the viewers in the lower-left corner of your own story to navigate to the post insights (see Figure 8-9).

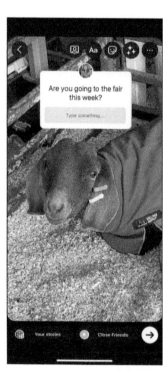

FIGURE 8-9:
Use the Question sticker to generate dialogue and participation with your followers. You'll be able to see their responses to your question.

Poll and Quiz stickers

Both the Poll and Quiz stickers work much the same as the Questions sticker. You can create a question and provide answer options for your audience to choose from. The polls results appear after the viewer has selected a response.

For the Quiz sticker, type in the question and then add answers. It defaults to two, but you can add more options. Tap the option for the correct response to highlight it (see Figure 8-10).

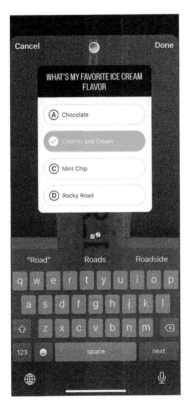

As with all stickers, pinch, drag, and move them where you want them in your story.

Chat sticker

The Chat sticker enables you to create a unique direct message thread exclusively for those who reply to the Chat sticker on your story.

When you add the sticker, followers can tap it to request to join the chat. When you approve them, they're added to the direct message thread along with anyone else you approve into the chat. You can stop the chat thread at any time by turning it off, and no one will be able to continue chatting in that conversation.

These chats are great for making weekend plans or coordinating a meetup with a group of people.

Link sticker

You may have heard of the "swipe up" link for Instagram Stories that allowed professional accounts to send viewers to a website URL. Well, now that's available for *all* users, regardless of the type of account or how many followers you have. You can add a Link to any story.

Select the Link sticker from the sticker options and then paste or type the URL into the field in the link screen. Then tap Done to add the sticker and place it anywhere on your story.

You can customize the link sticker text so that instead of defaulting to the website name in the sticker, you can say "Click here" or "Watch video." Simply tap on the + Customize Sticker Text option and type whatever custom text you want. See Figure 8-11.

Captions sticker for accessibility

A newer addition to stories is the Captions sticker. This sticker generates a transcript of the audio in your story. It is meant to increase accessibility, but it is also a helpful tool for users who like to view stories with the sound off.

Add the Captions sticker to your story and let the transcript process work its magic! The transcription is usually very good, but if you find a misspelled word, you can make edits by tapping the word before you tap Done. You can also choose from a few fonts by tapping the options at the bottom right of the screen. See Figure 8-12 for an example.

FIGURE 8-11:
Add a link to
a story and
label the link
with custom
text.

FIGURE 8-12:
The
Captions
sticker auto-
generates a
transcription
of the audio
in your
story.

If you'd like to turn on auto-generated captions for all the videos you watch throughout Instagram, follow these steps:

1. **From your Instagram profile page, tap the three lines at the top right.**

2. **Tap Settings.**

3. **Tap Account.**

4. **Tap Captions.**

5. **Toggle the Captions button to the right.**

Countdown and Music stickers to intrigue your followers

One of the best ways to keep your followers in the know about what you have going on is to use the Countdown sticker. For example, If you're hosting a party, going live on Instagram, leaving on vacation, or planning any other type of event, you can use the Countdown sticker to let people know when that event is going to happen. You can set a date and time for an upcoming event, and people can subscribe to the sticker to be notified when it expires.

The Music sticker may be one of the most sought-after stickers for most Instagram users. It's widely available, but was not rolled out to all accounts. For those that have it, it enables you to add a music overlay to any Story post.

You can choose from Instagram's music library (not your own) and add up to 15 seconds of music to an individual post. Select the Music sticker and navigate through the music options or search for a song or artist of your preference. Select the song by tapping it. Tap the number to the left of the slider to choose how long the music will play (between 5 and 15 seconds). Drag the slider to the clip of the song you want to use (see Figure 8-13).

Lyrics for the song appear on the screen. Slide through the Aa icons to choose the font option for the lyrics or choose one of the last options to display the song name or cover image instead of the lyrics.

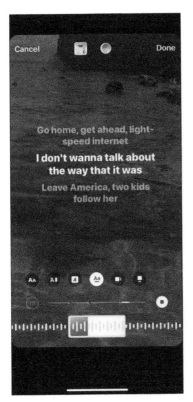

FIGURE 8-13:
The Music
sticker
allows you
to add a
music clip
of 5 to 15
seconds
onto a story
post.

Picture on picture for the fun of it

Another way to make your stories fun is to add a photo on top of your original photo or video story, as shown in Figure 8-14. Tap the smiley face at the top of the screen once you take/upload a photo or video. Select the photo icon sticker (a circle with your latest photo inside it) from the sticker screen.

You then get to choose another photo from your camera roll. Select the photo and place it over your original story. Then you can drag the photo around the screen and pinch to change the size, or tap it to get options to change its shape.

FIGURE 8-14:
Add a
picture-on-
picture
effect to
your stories
by using the
photo
sticker.

Stickers for causes

Instagram launched several stickers that support different causes — for example, COVID-19 vaccination, Shop Creators, Support Ukraine, Pride, and more. When you use one of these stickers on your story, it becomes part of a shared story with others who have used the sticker. Some stickers, like the COVID-19 vaccination sticker, link to further information about the cause. Figure 8-15 shows examples of stickers for causes.

Deleting stickers that don't work

It's easy to add stickers, and it's just as easy to remove them (before you post the story) if you don't like them. After you've added the sticker to your story, tap and hold the sticker; a garbage can appears at the bottom of the story screen (see Figure 8-16). Simply drag the sticker to the garbage can to remove it.

FIGURE 8-15:
Stickers for
causes show
your
support for
a cause and
group your
story with
others that
display that
sticker.

super
cute~

FIGURE 8-16:
Tap and
hold any
sticker in a
story to drag
it down to
the trash
can to
remove it
from your
post.

Personalizing Stories with Doodles

Instagram stories have a variety of drawing tools that enable you to add freehand doodles and scribbles. To access the drawing tools, tap the three dots at the top of the story screen and then tap Draw (see Figure 8-17).

FIGURE 8-17: Tap the three dots at the top right of the screen to access the drawing tools.

Instagram offers a variety of pen and drawing tools along the top of the screen. Each pen creates a different effect, from a simple pen/pencil to a highlighter, an eraser, and more.

On the left side of the screen is a sizing tool. You can drag the dot up and down to make the drawing tool thicker or thinner. Color options are along the bottom of the screen. You can scroll left and right along the color option bar to access more color selections (see Figure 8-18).

FIGURE 8-18:
Doodle tools offer different pen, thickness, and color options.

TIP

You can also get really creative and choose any color of the rainbow rather than just the listed color options. Tap and hold any color circle on the row of colors to see the whole spectrum of colors; then just drag your finger to find the perfect shade.

If you want to match a specific color, you can tap the eyedropper tool next to the color palette and then tap the item in your image that you want to match. That color becomes your pen color.

TIP

If you want to fill the screen with a certain color, choose the standard pen tool, pick the color of your choice, and then tap and hold the screen. The color you chose fills the entire screen, creating a blank canvas to work on.

When you're done with any doodle, tap Done to save it to your story.

While you're adding doodles, you may want to undo something you've drawn. Simply tap the Undo link to undo the last doodle you created. You can keep undoing all the way back to the first one you added. However, once you've tapped the check mark to apply the doodles, you can't undo them.

Saying More with Text

A picture may be worth a thousand words, but sometimes you may want to personalize your stories with some text.

To access the Text option, tap the Aa icon in the top toolbar when creating your story or simply tap anywhere on the screen to open the text tool.

You can add multiple text boxes to your story and place them wherever you choose. Pinch a text box to change the size and rotate it as you please.

Changing your font option

The font option defaults to a basic font. You can change this easily to one of the other font options by scrolling through the options at the middle of the screen, as shown in the middle image in Figure 8-19.

You In addition to font choices, you can choose different colors for your fonts by tapping the multicolored circle at the top of the screen and choosing a color. To change the justification from left- to center- to right-justified, tap the alignment icon in the upper-left corner of the screen.

You can also add background colors or fill the text box with a color. If you see the "A**" icon, that lets you know that option is available. Tapping the "A**" icon fills the text box with the selected color, but you can change it by tapping a color palette of the options.

Removing your text boxes

REMEMBER

You can easily remove text boxes (before saving changes) if you decide you don't want them. Simply tap and hold to reveal the trash can icon and drag the text box onto the trash can to remove it.

Chapter **9**

Being Sneaky with Sharing Stories

Sometimes you want to use content that someone else created or you want to repurpose your own content for your stories. In this chapter, we show you how to share, or repost, Instagram stories to your own, how to reuse existing content, and how to be selective in who you share your stories with.

Sharing Another Story to Your Own Story

You may come across a cool Instagram story that you want to share to your own stories. Unfortunately, you can't directly share just any story to your own. There isn't an existing tool within Instagram that allows this. There are, however, two workarounds:

>> **If you're tagged in someone's story, you can share that story to your own.** If a friend of yours posts a story and includes your username tag in the post, you receive a notification in your direct messages. Included with the notification that you were mentioned in their story is the Add to Your Story option (see Figure 9-1).

When you tap that option, you initiate a story post where their post appears in the screen. You can shrink or enlarge it, reposition it, and add your own content to it using stickers, doodles, and more.

>> **You can take a screen shot of another person's story, saving it as an image.** It should be pretty obvious that this only works well with photos, not videos. When you have the screen shot of their story, you can upload that image as your own story.

WARNING

Taking a screen shot and reposting it does put you in the area of copyright infringement, and you never want to use someone's post without their permission. Always ask them first if you have their permission to repost it. You can send them a direct message or reply to their story to ask for that permission.

FIGURE 9-1:
The option to share someone else's story post to your own story.

Sharing Some Stories to Select People

For all the fun you can have creating Instagram stories, you may not want every post to be available to every one of your followers or to anyone publicly. Fortunately, Instagram has provided a few solutions to allow you to send stories privately or to select groups of people.

Sharing via a direct message

If you want to share a story post to one or a number of individuals via a direct message, you can easily do so. Create your story as you normally would, adding all your personalized components.

At the bottom of the screen, tap the Share button (the white button that contains a black arrow) instead of the Your Story button (see Figure 9-2). In the Share menu, tap Message. A new screen opens with a list of people you commonly send messages to.

If the person you want to send it to is listed there, simply tap the Send button next to their name and they'll receive the story in their direct messages. You can repeat this process to send the same story to more than one person using this method.

TIP

If the person you want to send it to is not listed, use the Search bar to type in the person's name and then select who to send the story to.

Sharing to your Close Friends list

You may have noticed that there is also an option to send stories to your Close Friends list. This feature is a messaging tool that allows you to select a number of the people you follow on Instagram and put them into a group called Close Friends.

To set up your list of close friends, go to your Instagram profile and tap the three-line button in the upper-right corner. The Menu page appears, where you can tap Close Friends to select and set up your list (see Figure 9-3).

FIGURE 9-2:
The Share
button is in
the
lower-right
corner of
the screen.

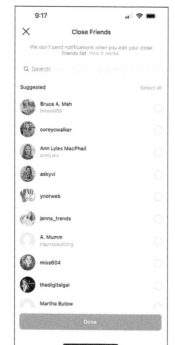

FIGURE 9-3:
Navigate to
the menu
tab on your
profile to
access the
Close
Friends tab
to set up a
list of
friends.

In the Close Friends screen, you see a list of recommended friends, based on those you most often interact with. You can add any of them by tapping the circle button next to their names (see Figure 9-4). If the person or people you want to add are not listed in the suggestions, you can use the search bar to type the name of the person you follow and add them to your list.

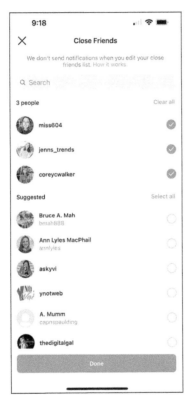

FIGURE 9-4:
Tap the circle next to a person's name to add a check mark and put the person on your Close Friends list.

You can add multiple people to this list, but you can only have one list. You may want to use this list for family, friends, or colleagues.

If you add someone by accident or you later want to remove someone from the list, navigate back to this Close Friends list and tap to remove the check mark next to the name of the person.

Once you have your Close Friends list set up, tap Done. Now you can share stories specifically with them!

When you're in your story creation screen (see Figure 9-5), you can tap the Close Friends icon at the bottom of the screen to share it with the list, or you can tap the Share button and choose the Close Friends list from the next screen.

Close Friends button

FIGURE 9-5: Easily share a story to your Close Friends list by tapping the Close Friends icon.

Sharing Instagram Posts and Reels to Your Stories

As creative and unique as Instagram stories are, you may want to share an Instagram post or a Reel to a story. A good educational piece, a post about news or something trendy, or even just good entertainment can be worthy of sharing with your followers.

Instagram has provided a simple sharing tool that you can use to share a post to your story. Under any feed post or in any Reel (your own or someone else's) is a paper airplane icon (see Figure 9-6). This is the share icon.

Share icon

FIGURE 9-6:
Use the paper airplane icon to share a post on Instagram.

Tap the share icon to open a screen that allows you to choose how you want to share that post. To share it to your story, simply tap the Add Post to Your Story option, as shown on the left in Figure 9-7.

This will open your story creation screen with the image of that post or the first part of the video added to the story. If sharing a feed post image, when you tap the image of the original post, you can toggle between two display options, one with just the original image and the account's username (as shown on the right in Figure 9-7), or a screenshot of the original post, including the first couple lines of the caption.

You can edit the story, moving the post image or adding text, doodles, and stickers. When the story is published, the post image is a hyperlink back to the original post so others can view it.

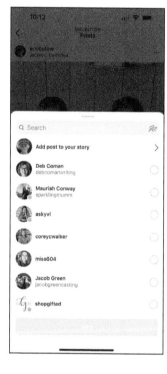

FIGURE 9-7: Sharing a post to your story creates a hyperlinked image back to the original post that your followers can tap on to view the original post.

If you don't see the option to share to your story, that means the person who published the original story hasn't allowed their followers to share it.

TIP

Some of your followers may only watch your stories and not regularly see your feed posts. If you have a great piece of content you uploaded to your Instagram account, but you want to make sure people who watch your stories see it too, you can share your own post to your story. Go to the post on your own profile that you want to share, and follow the instructions earlier to share the post to your story.

Changing Your Story into a Regular Instagram Post

In the reverse of sharing posts to stories, you might create an incredible Instagram story and want to share that to your regular feed. Yes, you can do that, too!

Open any story, current or archived, and tap the three-dot More button in the lower-right corner of the story post (see Figure 9-8). A screen appears with a variety of options, including Share as Post. Tap that option and the post opens in a regular Instagram feed upload screen.

FIGURE 9-8: Convert an Instagram story into a feed post on your profile by tapping the More button on any current or archived story post and choosing to share it as a post.

If your story post was a static image, it transfers to the feed post as an image. Any stickers, text, or doodles, remain on the image. If your story post was a video or included animated stickers like GIFs, the post will upload to your feed as a video, retaining those features.

Any interactive components like polls, sliders, and chat stickers don't retain their functionality in the feed post. They simply appear as static stickers.

Because stories are uploaded at a 9:16 dimension, you have to edit the image orientation and sizing of the feed post to select the area of the story you want to showcase. You can't display the full 9:16 original post. An Instagram feed post has a maximum ratio of 4:5.

After uploading the story post and arranging it for the right orientation, continue editing the post, adding a caption, and adding any other components as you would to upload any other Instagram post.

Chapter **10**

Using Instagram Highlights to Keep Your Content Alive

Stories disappear after 24 hours, and it can be frustrating to know that the content you created is lost. However, there's a way you can keep those stories alive longer. Highlights allow you to select certain stories to stay active on your profile in specific galleries you set up.

In this chapter, we explain how to set up highlights and how to add content to them. We also talk about some of the reasons why you may want to use highlights and give you some creative ideas for highlight topics.

Getting Acquainted with Highlights

Story Highlights are the series of circles directly beneath a person's bio on their Instagram profile (see Figure 10-1). A person may only have a few of these galleries, or they may have a number of them that you can scroll through.

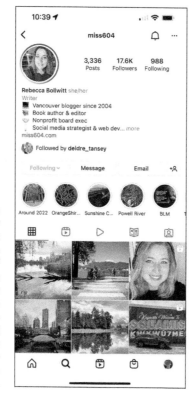

FIGURE 10-1: Story Highlights are the series of circles beneath the bio and are a place to collect stories you want to live more than 24 hours.

Each highlight gallery is a collection of stories from that account. Each highlight may contain only one story post or multiple story posts from various times.

A story disappears from the account after 24 hours, but highlights are an opportunity to keep that content on your profile for as long as you want it there.

You can customize all the highlights for your own profile with whatever topics and titles you like!

Creating a New Highlight Gallery

Story Highlights are available to all users, but you have to have active or archived stories on your profile to have access to adding a highlight gallery. If you've never shared a story before, go ahead and create one! That opens the option to add highlights to your profile.

If you have access to highlights, the Story Highlights section is beneath the bio information on your profile. If you haven't yet created any highlights, the circles will be gray and you'll see a circle with a plus sign (+) to create a new highlight.

Adding a highlight from your profile

To create a new highlight from your profile, tap the plus sign (+) in the circle below your bio. A list of your archived stories appears (see Figure 10-2). Scroll through the list of posts and select one or more you want to add to that highlight.

Tap Next after you've selected your posts and move on to the "Naming and customizing your highlight" section.

Adding a highlight from an active story

If you have an active story on your profile and you want to use that one to create a new highlight, you can easily do that by opening the story post from your profile or feed.

At the bottom of your story post is a variety of buttons, including the Highlight button, which is a circle with a heart in the center (see Figure 10-3). Tap that icon, and then proceed to the next section for instructions for naming and customizing your highlight.

FIGURE 10-2:
When starting a new Story Highlights gallery, you'll be able to choose from your archived stories which post(s) to add to the highlight.

FIGURE 10-3:
When you access your active stories, you'll see the Highlight icon (the circle with the heart in the center), which allows you to add that active story to a highlight gallery.

Highlight icon

Naming and customizing your highlight

Now that you've started a highlight, you need to give it a name. A cursor blinks underneath the cover image so you can type the name. Before you do, here are some things to be aware of:

>> Highlight titles can be up to 15 characters in length.

>> The titles get cut off after a handful of characters (there's no set limit).

>> Keep the titles as short as possible and keep the most important info at the start of the title.

Type your highlight title and tap Add to create the new Highlight on your profile. What happens next depends on whether you're adding a highlight from your profile or an active story:

>> **If you're adding a highlight from your profile,** then your profile page appears so you can see your added highlight.

>> **If you're adding a highlight from an active story,** the Added to Highlights pop-up screen appears. In this screen, tap View on Profile to see your highlight in your profile. Close the screen by tapping Done.

Adding Content to a Highlight

After you get your highlights set up, you may want to keep adding content to them. Here, we walk you through the steps to add and delete content from a highlight.

Sharing a current story

If you have an active story on your profile that you want to add to an existing highlight, you simply have to access that story from your profile and tap the Highlight icon (refer to Figure 10-3) just as you would when creating a new highlight.

Scroll through the list of highlights and select the one you want to add the story to. Tap that highlight cover image, and your story will be added to the highlight.

Finding an archived story

To add more content to an existing highlight, you can also select from older, archived stories.

The first option is to tap the highlight on your profile. When you're in the highlight, tap the three-dot Menu button and tap Edit Highlight. You can then select the Add tab (on Android devices) or the Stories tab (on iOS devices) to scroll through archived stories and select as many as you want to add to that highlight (see Figure 10-4).

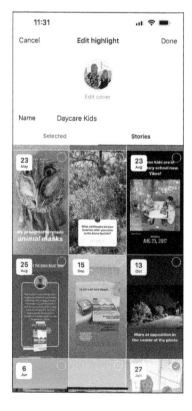

FIGURE 10-4: Add archived stories to a highlight from the Edit Highlight option on any existing highlight by tapping the Add tab (Android) or the Stories tab (iOS) and selecting the story posts to include.

Alternatively, you can go into your archived stories by tapping the three-line button on your profile screen and selecting Archive from the menu page (see the image on the left in Figure 10-5) to view all your old stories in that feed. Select any story from the list (shown in the image on the right in Figure 10-5) and tap the Highlight icon at the bottom of the story to add it to a highlight.

FIGURE 10-5:
Add archived stories to a highlight by accessing the archived stories from your profile and adding each one to a highlight.

Deleting a story from a highlight

If, at some point, you decide you no longer want a particular story to appear in your highlight gallery, you can easily remove it.

Select the highlight from your profile and advance through the story posts in the highlight until you arrive at the one you want to remove. Tap the three-dot Menu button in the lower right. Tap Remove from Highlight from the pop-up screen (see Figure 10-6), and confirm that you want to remove that item from the highlight.

If you want to delete a bulk number of story posts, you can tap the three-dot Menu button, tap Edit Highlight, and uncheck all the story posts from the list. Tap Done to save the changes, which removes those stories from the highlight.

Coming Up with Fun Ideas for Highlights

You can use highlights for any topic that you create with your stories! It's best to group your stories into specific topics for your highlights, though.

For example, you may have a lot of stories of your family. But you could create one highlight for family vacations, another one for holiday celebrations, and another one for just your pets.

TIP

You can have plenty of different highlights, so feel free to use them as best suited for you. Just realize that only the four most recently used highlights appear on the profile. After that, users have to scroll to see your other highlight galleries.

Chapter **11**

Going Live on Instagram

Quickly after they launched, Instagram stories dramatically changed the way people used Instagram. Given the popularity of stories, a live video option in Instagram stories seemed like a natural next step.

In this chapter, you find out how to go live and get tips for making your live broadcast more successful before, during, and after filming.

Getting Started with Live Videos

So, you're ready to go live, but how do you even get to it? How do you use it? Its location is not exactly obvious. Follow these steps:

1. **Open Instagram stories by swiping right or using the camera icon at the top of the newsfeed.**

2. **At the bottom of the screen, swipe Story to the left so you're on Live or tap on the + icon at the top of the screen and choose Live.**

   Figure 11-1a shows the Instagram Live screen.

3. **When you're ready to start, tap the shutter button with the live icon.**

   Instagram checks your connection, and then you're on! You'll begin seeing *Username* Has Joined and the number of people who have joined.

4. **Wait a minute or two before diving into your topic so that people have time to join.**

   Greet as many people as possible. Say hi, calling them by their names or usernames. Make them feel welcome.

5. **While you're live, you can do the following:**

   - Turn off comments by tapping the three dots in the comment bubble and then choosing the option to turn off from the pop-up screen, as shown in the center in Figure 11-1. However, we recommend that you keep them turned on for more interaction.

   - Add a face filter by tapping the face with stars icon.

   - Turn the camera from the front-facing selfie camera to the rear-facing camera to showcase what you're seeing rather than showing your face. Tap the curved double arrow (shown on the left in Figure 11-1) to change the camera view.

   - Enter the name of your live broadcast by typing it in a comment and tapping Send. Then tap the comment and choose Pin Comment from the options menu. This pins the name to the top of the comment feed, where it acts like a title.

   - To keep track of your time, tap the Live button in the upper right. A timer appears.

   - To see the names of the people who have joined, tap the number to the right of the pink Live button. To kick people out of your Live broadcast, place an X by their name.

FIGURE 11-1:
Go live on
Instagram
(left), turn off
commenting
or questions
(center), and
save and
share your
live video
(right.

6. **When you're finished, tap the X in the upper-right corner, and then tap End Video.**

7. **After you end the video, you can view insights from the broadcast (including viewers reached, video shares, and more) plus save the live video to your device or share it to your feed (shown on the right in Figure 11-1).**

   To view the video performance metrics, tap View Insights in the pop-up menu shown in Figure 11-1c.

8. **To save the video to your device, tap View in Live Archive, select the recent video in the live archive screen by tapping it, and then tap the Download icon in the lower-right corner of the video viewer (refer to right image in Figure 11-1).**

WARNING

   You must have enough storage space on your mobile device to save the full video. If you don't have enough storage space, only a portion or even none of the video will save.

9. **To share the live video with your Instagram followers, tap Share from the pop-up screen after ending the live video (refer to the right image in Figure 11-1).**

   A new post screen opens to enable you to post the live video on your feed with a caption and tags, as shown in Figure 11-2.

WARNING

Instagram Live has a four-hour time limit. You'll see a 15-second timer countdown when your time is almost up, and then the live broadcast ends. If possible, plan your schedule accordingly so as not to exceed that limit.

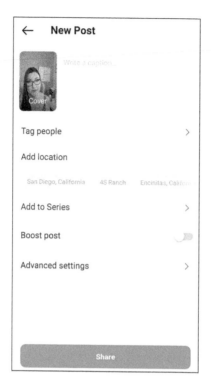

FIGURE 11-2:
After you
complete
your new
post, share
your post by
tapping the
Share
button.

Developing a Game Plan

TIP

Now that you know how to physically tap all the buttons to record a live broadcast, it's time to talk strategy. We recommend going on Instagram Live with forethought about what you'll be doing. Here are a few tips to help you execute the best Instagram Live possible:

>> **Think of a topic that will interest your followers.** Some ideas to consider: Showcase your family life, stream your child's rehearsal, show off some of your vacation, share a holiday tradition.

>> **If you plan to talk on the live broadcast, jot down several talking points, but don't memorize or look overly rehearsed.** Live broadcasts are supposed to be a bit off the cuff.

>> **If possible, do a test video on your regular camera app where you plan to do the live broadcast, and at the same time of day.** Check the lighting and the background. Make sure that you can get a decent signal in that location.

>> **Promote your live broadcast ahead of time.** You can post about it in your Instagram stories, on Facebook, and on other social media.

>> **Be as interactive as possible with your followers during the broadcast.** You can ask them questions in the chat, give a live tutorial to spark questions, or have your followers ask you questions in the comments so you can answer them verbally.

>> **Save your broadcast so you can repurpose it to other online media, and then publish your broadcast so it's available for 24 hours. (We talk about cross-posting photos to Facebook in Chapter 3.)**

TIP

It's often helpful to have a tripod to hold your camera steady and in place while filming live. Arkon Mounts (www.arkon.com) has several tripods available for less than $50.

Inviting Guests onto Your Live Broadcast

If being live on camera alone makes you nervous, or if you just want to include someone else in your video, Instagram allows you to invite up to three guests into the live show with you.

If guests have requested to join your livestream, tap the video camera icon with the + sign at the bottom of the live video screen and you'll see the list of names. You can then add that user to the live video. Or, if you want to invite someone to join the live with you, tap the icon with the person and the right-facing arrow (next to the camera with the + sign) and type the name of the user you want to add or select them from the suggested list (see Figure 11-3).

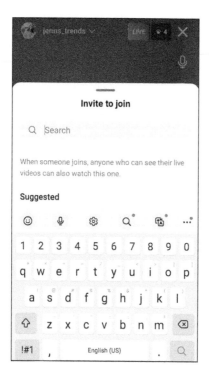

FIGURE 11-3:
Inviting
people to
join your live
video.

When a single guest joins you on the live video, they'll occupy half the screen, sharing their video and audio. If you have two guests, you'll be in the upper half and they'll split the lower half. If you have three guests, each person will have a quarter of the full screen.

Scheduling a Live Broadcast

If you want to go live in the future but not right now, you can schedule your live broadcast. On the iPhone, tap the calendar icon on the left side of the screen (refer to left image in Figure 11-1). In Android, tap on the + icon, choose the Live option, and then select the calendar icon to schedule the video. You'll need to assign a video title and pick the start time and date. Then tap Schedule Live Video (iPhone) or Schedule Live (Android) to set up the scheduled broadcast, as shown in Figure 11-4.

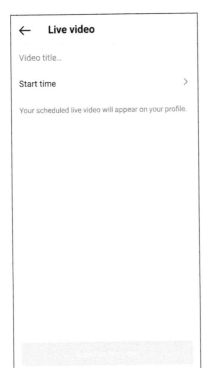

FIGURE 11-4:
Tap Video
Title at the
top of the
Live Video
screen to
name your
saved video.

5

Becoming a Pro at Reels

Chapter **12**

Understanding Reels

The Instagram Reels feature, which rolled out to the majority of users in August 2020, is a response to the popularity of TikTok and a way to create similar content in the Instagram platform.

Reels, like Instagram stories, are built into the existing Instagram interface. You can even access the reels camera from the Story screen. In this chapter, we talk about viewing reels, and in Chapter 13 we get into the details of creating reels.

Finding and Watching Reels

Chances are you've seen reels on Instagram already, even if you didn't realize it. Reels can be uploaded to stories, your feed, a reels gallery on your profile, and even shown on the Explore page. They're pretty much everywhere!

You can recognize a Reels video as you're scrolling through your feed because it will have a play button inside a clapboard icon in the lower-left corner of the video. If you're looking at someone's Instagram profile, the icon is in the upper-right corner, as shown in Figure 12-1.

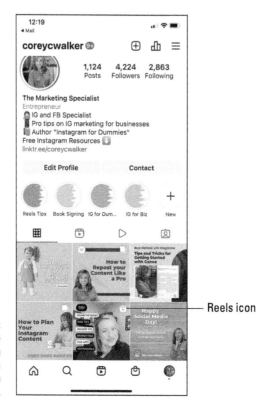

Reels icon

FIGURE 12-1:
The Instagram Reel has a Reels icon in the post.

If a reels video has been uploaded to the feed of someone you follow, you'll see the video in your home feed and also on the person's profile. If the person didn't share the reels video to the feed, a Reels tab on the profile displays uploaded videos, as shown in Figure 12-2.

In addition to seeing the reels of people you follow or accounts you visit, you can find new reels in the Explore page. When you go to the Explore page, a Reels video is selected for you at the top of the page. As you scroll through the Explore feed, you see more Reels videos interspersed as vertical videos and labeled with the Reels icon, as shown in Figure 12-3.

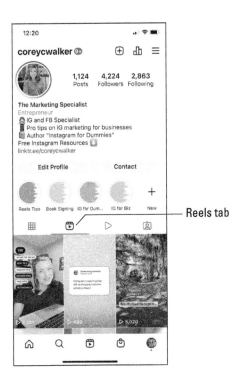

Reels tab

FIGURE 12-2:
Instagram
Reels have a
tab on the
account
profile page.

FIGURE 12-3:
Instagram
Reels are
discoverable
in the
Explore
feed.

After you view one video from the Explore feed or from your home feed, you can swipe up to scroll through more videos in Reels and find fun new content from other creators.

If you only want to see reels, tap the Reels icon in the bottom menu bar to go to the dedicated Reels feed, where you can see a mix of suggested content and videos from Instagram users you follow. You'll be taken to a video that you can then watch or swipe up to see the next one.

Tapping into Whose Videos You're Seeing

If you watch reels from the Reels tab or the Explore page, you are shown videos of people you don't necessarily follow. Using an algorithm based on other accounts you follow, like, and comment on, Instagram presents more reels it thinks you may enjoy (see Figure 12-4).

FIGURE 12-4: Instagram shows you reels it thinks you will enjoy on the Reels and Explore tabs.

Tap to see audio information

From this screen, you can do a variety of things:

» Tap the user name to visit their profile.

» Tap Follow to follow them and see their reels in your feed.

» Like the reel by tapping the heart or double-tapping the video.

» Leave a comment by tapping the bubble, writing a message, and tapping Post.

» Add the reel to your story or send it as a DM to someone else by tapping the paper airplane.

» Tap the three dots at the top right to share the reel to apps outside of Instagram, copy the link to share it elsewhere, save the reel, remix the reel with your own clip, create a shareable QR code, or report a user's content for being offensive, untrue, or illegal so that Instagram can review it. (See Figure 12-5.)

» Tap the box on the bottom right (refer to Figure 12-4) to view the audio used in the reel (see Figure 12-6).

FIGURE 12-5:
Tap the three dots to reveal several more reels options.

FIGURE 12-6:
Tap the box at the bottom right to view and save the audio used in the reel.

IN THIS CHAPTER

» **Getting ready to create reels**

» **Uploading videos**

» **Editing your reel**

» **Sharing your reel with others**

» **Using Reels Insights**

Chapter **13**

Creating a Reels Presence

As mentioned in Chapter 12, the Instagram Reels feature was rolled out to keep up with TikTok's rapidly growing audience. As such, much of the functionality of Instagram Reels is similar to TikTok. In this chapter, we go over how to gather ideas, upload and record reels, edit reels, and share them with your audience.

Doing the Preproduction Work

Crafting a well-produced reel that gets many views takes some planning. First, you need to know a little about the specs of reels, and then you need to plan what kind of content you're going to have in your reels.

Reels are short-form video content, in full 9:16 portrait mode, and they can be up to 90 seconds long. When you create reels, you can

>> Film them directly in the Reels camera or upload them from your camera roll on your mobile device

>> Film them as one full take or a series of takes stitched together

>> View them on mobile devices or from a desktop computer

The way you create the reel depends on your intention. So the first step for gathering ideas for reels is to set your intentions. Are you doing them for fun, promoting your business, trying to become an influencer, sharing a hobby, or educating people?

Once you set your intention, start watching the accounts that have a similar intention and pay attention to what draws you in. Make a list of the attributes that attract you to that content, which may be things such as the following:

>> Trending audio clips

>> Dance moves

>> Humor

>> Transitions

>> Text overlays

Think about how you can incorporate the things you like into a reel that is unique to you!

Recording and Uploading Videos to Reels

Recording and uploading reels is not unlike uploading other videos to Instagram. Here's how to get started:

1. **Open Instagram Reels by swiping right on the newsfeed then swiping left in the menu to select Reel or by tapping the + sign at the top of the newsfeed and then tapping Reel.**

2. **Make sure the setting at the bottom of the screen is set to Reel before you record.**

   To film a reel, you want to hold your phone vertically.

TIP

3. **Change settings by tapping the appropriate icon located on the left side of the reels screen, as shown in Figure 13-1.**

   You have to select your settings before you record. Except for audio, you can't go back and add or edit clips for the following features after you've recorded them:

   - **Audio** (music note icon): Search for an audio file to add to your reel. The saved audio will be available to you under the Music Note when you create a Reel under a button called Saved.

   - **Effects** (three-stars icon): Scroll through the various filters available to the left and right of the reels camera button to enhance your image. (This may also appear above the white record button for some users.)

   - **Length** (icon showing 15 within a circle): Choose a 15-, 30-, 60-, or 90-second length for your reel.

   - **Speed** (1x icon): Open a menu and select from one of six speed settings. The default is 1x.

   - **Layouts** (Square with a rectangle and two squares icon): Open the Layout feature and choose different layouts for your reel.

   - **Timer** (stopwatch icon): Open the Timer window to set the timer for hands-free recording.

   - **Dual** (camera icon): Allows you to record both your forward-facing and selfie-facing view on the same reel as a picture in picture.

4. **Record your clip by tapping and holding down on the white circle button at the bottom of the screen.**

   You can record up to 90 seconds (if the 90-second button is chosen). As you record, a red line circles around the white camera button indicating your progress.

Audio

Length

Speed

Layout

Timer

Dual

Scroll through filters

FIGURE 13-1:
The setting
icons appear
on the left
side of the
Reels
screen.

5. **Add more than one clip by recording using the white button, letting go, and then pressing the white button again to record another clip.**

   You can shoot as many clips as you want as long as they total less than 90 seconds (or whichever time you selected). When you record multiple clips, you'll notice breaks in the red circle indicating the start of each new clip as shown in Figure 13-2.

If you have previously recorded vertical video, you can also upload videos from your camera roll. The platform supports videos, images, or graphics. To access your camera roll, tap the square with the blue + sign in the lower-left corner of the screen (refer to Figure 13-2). Then tap the content you want to upload from the camera roll screen. If you upload a video longer than 90 seconds or longer than the amount of time left in your current reels video, the uploaded video is trimmed to the allowed time. Select the portion of the video to upload and tap the Add button in the upper-right corner of the screen to add it to your Reels creation. If you want to add several videos, repeat the steps and continue to click Add, you'll see how much time is left in the progress bar around the white button (iPhone) or a progress bar across the top (Android).

FIGURE 13-2:
A red circle shows the progress of your recording.

WARNING

Make sure you choose the correct amount of time for your reel from the start when recording. If you choose a 15-second reel, and you film a longer video, the video gets trimmed at the 15-second mark. This does not apply to uploads, however, as long as they are under the max of 90 seconds.

Adding Finesse to Your Reels

There are many fun ways to edit and enhance your reels. You can add audio, trim your videos to show only certain parts of a video in a reel, add text, and include transitions between sections of the video.

Finding trending audio

Using trending audio that's on the rise (versus overplayed) is a great way to get more views on your reel. There are a few ways you can find trending audio:

» Watch a bunch of reels and take note of which audio clips you hear the most. You can find out the name of the audio by looking at the bottom left of the screen when you are watching reels in the reels section (not your main feed). Trending audio will also have an arrow pointing up next to the name of the audio. (See Figure 13-3.)

• To save the audio for later use, tap the name of the audio clip or tap the square at the bottom right of the screen while watching the Reel. Find out more about adding audio to a reel in the "Recording and Uploading Videos to Your Reels" section earlier in this chapter.

• On the next screen, tap Save Audio. You can also watch other Reels in this area that have used this same audio. This is an easy way to get some new ideas!

» You can also find audio that Instagram is suggesting for you by going to create a Reel and tapping on the music note icon at the top of the menu on the left. Doing so shows you a For You area (see Figure 13-4) to choose from.

» Visit tokboard.com/ to find TikTok trending audio. (TikTok tends to take the lead on trending audio, and then it migrates over to Instagram days to weeks later, so the trendiest audio can often be found on TikTok first.) The site lists the top songs of the week on TikTok, along with the audio clip so you can listen to it right there. If you find an audio clip you like, take note of the name of it and then search for it under the Music Note when you create your next Reel.

Audio information

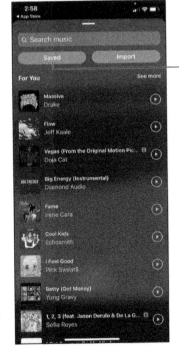

Saved audio

Trimming and deleting clips

Once you've recorded or uploaded a video clip as a reel, you can easily trim your clips as needed:

1. **Record or upload your video(s) to Reels as described in the earlier section of this chapter.**

2. **Replay the clip(s) by tapping the Next button.**

3. **Trim the clip(s) by tapping the Edit Clips button in the bottom left of the screen and tapping the clip you want to edit (if there are multiple clips).**

4. **Use the handles on either side of the clip to trim the clip, as shown in Figure 13-5.**

5. **When you're finished, tap the clip that's on screen to go back to your main screen or click on the All Clips button under your clip to go back and view all of them.**

   In the editing screen, you can also reorder multiple clips by tapping and holding on to them, then sliding them left or right, or delete the entire clip by tapping the Delete button.

FIGURE 13-5: Trim the clip by sliding the handles on either side of your clip.

Adding and timing text

Reels often include text to let users know what the reel is about. Follow these instructions to add text and synchronize the text to particular parts of the video:

1. Record or upload a video in Reels; then tap Next.

2. Tap the Aa icon on the top of the screen, and start typing.

3. Change the fonts by scrolling through the available fonts above the keyboard.

4. Change the color of the text by tapping the color wheel at the top of the screen, then choosing a color (see Figure 13-6).

FIGURE 13-6: Change the text color by choosing from the available colors above the keyboard.

5. Change the background of the text by tapping the A at the middle of the top of the screen.

6. Make the text move on the screen by tapping the A that looks like it's in motion.

7. Tap Done once the text is the way you'd like it.

8. At the bottom of the screen, you see a repeat of your text in an oval (see Figure 13-7). Tap that, and use the white handles at either end of the video to place the text on the correct spot of the video.

9. Tap Next to go to the Share screen, or tap the back arrow in the top left of your screen to upload or record more clips.

TIP

You can also add stickers, polls, location information, GIFs and more to a reel. These capabilities, which are the same for stories and reels, are covered in-depth in Chapter 8.

FIGURE 13-7: Use the white handles to choose the timing of your text overlay on the video.

Creating a transition

A transition is an effect that helps you move from one scene to the next or grab someone's attention. There are manual ways to create a transition, but the easiest way is to use one of the effects (filters) offered within reels. The effect will often direct you to do something, like move your ahead to trigger the transition effect.

Popular transition effects include the following:

>> Warp

>> Spin

>> Scan

>> Zoom

>> Duplicate

>> Selfie Skit

>> Body Dynamic

>> Freeze Frame

Here's how to access them:

1. Open Instagram stories by swiping right then swiping left in the menu at the bottom to select Reel, or by tapping the + sign and then tapping Reel at the top of the newsfeed.

2. Make sure the setting at the bottom of the new screen is set to Reel and that your phone is in the vertical orientation.

3. Tap Effects on the left side of your screen (iPhone) or above the white record button (Android) (see Figure 13-8).

4. In the magnifying glass area located at the left of the effects screen, type in Transition.

5. Tap on a transition effect and it will be applied as a filter to your reel (see Figure 13-9).

6. Record your video using that transition. The effect should have a simple instruction with it to show you how it works.

Effects

FIGURE 13-8:
Tap Effects on the
left-hand side of
the Reels creation
screen.

FIGURE 13-9:
Scroll through the
effects and
choose the one
you'd like to use.

Using the New Reel (Share) Screen to its Full Potential

When you have your reel the way you want it, you're ready to share it with the world. At the bottom right of the reels screen (you will see Edit Clips at the bottom left), tap Next to access the New Reel screen, and then use these steps:

1. **Use any of the following features to enhance your reel if you'd like:**

    *   **Change the cover photo:** Tap the cover thumbnail image and then tap an image at the bottom of the screen to select a frame from the reel. You can also add an image from your camera roll (iOS) or gallery (Android), as shown in Figure 13-10.

FIGURE 13-10: Tap the cover image to select a frame from the video, or upload an image from your camera roll (iOS) or gallery (Android).

- **Adjust the profile photo:** On the Edit Cover screen tap the Profile Grid tab (see Figure 13-11). You can drag the photo within the cropping box to select the view that will be shown on your profile page. Tap Done when you are finished.

2:34

Cancel   **Edit cover**   Done

Cover   **Profile grid**

Drag to edit crop

FIGURE 13-11:
Edit the profile photo by dragging it within the cropping square.

- **Write a caption:** Tap in the Write a caption box that appears below the thumbnail of your reel and then type your caption. As with a feed post, you can write up to 2,200 characters and 30 hashtags.

- **Tag people:** Tap on the arrow to add a tag, or invite someone to collaborate with you. (Read more about collaborating in the "Collabing with a friend" section later in this chapter.)

- **Rename audio:** Tap on the arrow and enter a new name for your audio; then tap Done.

- **Add location:** Tap on the arrow and then search for the location to tag, or tap one of the locations listed below the search bar.

- **Add Fundraiser** (may not be available to all users yet): Tap the arrow and choose a nonprofit by searching or choosing a nonprofit from the list. You can also choose a goal donation amount and ask others to collaborate.

- **Recommend on Facebook:** Tap the arrow to set whether the reel will also be shown on Facebook Reels. When the button is toggled to blue, the reel may be shown to users watching reels on Facebook.

TIP

If you're not ready to share the post publicly, tap Save Draft at the bottom of the screen to save the video file so you can edit it later. To access a saved draft, open your Instagram profile and tap the Reels icon directly above the grid of posts. Any drafts you have will appear at the top left of your other draft thumbnails. Tap Drafts to see your available drafts. In the Reels Drafts screen, tap the thumbnail image for the video to access it.

2. **To share your reel to Instagram Reels tap Share (see Figure 13-12).**

   If you'd also like to share the reel to your Instagram feed, make sure the Also Share to Feed option is toggled to blue; otherwise, it will only be shown in the reels feed and on your profile.

Collabing with a friend

Sometimes two heads are better than one. Grab a friend, either close by or far away, to do a collaboration, also known as a "collab." Instagrammers often collab from completely different places, each creating part of a reel and then splicing it together during the editing process. We discuss more about editing earlier in the chapter in the "Adding Finesse to Your Reels" section.

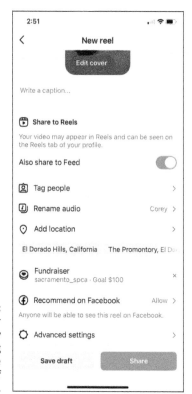

New reel screen showing caption field, Edit cover, Share to Reels, Also share to Feed toggle, Tag people, Rename audio (Corey), Add location, El Dorado Hills California / The Promontory, Fundraiser (sacramento_spca · Goal $100), Recommend on Facebook (Allow), Advanced settings, Save draft and Share buttons.

FIGURE 13-12:
Share your reel by tapping Share at the bottom of the screen.

A collab is also used widely by influencers. The influencer may be the only person filming the reel, but they can tag another person or business by selecting the Tag People option on the New Reel screen (see Figure 13-13) to collaborate with them. Then select Invite Collaborator (see Figure 13-14) to send a notification to whom you'd like to collaborate. The person tagged gets a notification about the request for the collaboration, and if they accept, the reel gets shown on both accounts.

Remixing a Reel

Remix is a video-editing feature that allows you to collab with another user to film reactionary reels that appear side by side with the original reel. You can remix any Instagram reel, as long as the original creator has enabled Remix access.

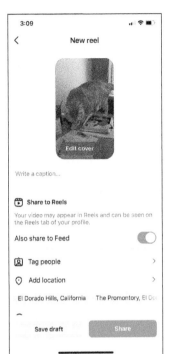

FIGURE 13-13:
Choose Tag
People and
tag the
person or
business you
want to
collaborate
with.

FIGURE 13-14:
Choose Invite
Collaborator
to send an
invitation to
the person
with whom
you'd like to
collaborate.

To allow others to remix your reel, do the following:

1. **Go to the three lines at the top of your profile page.**

2. **Tap Settings.**

3. **Tap Privacy.**

4. **Tap Reels and Remix.**

5. **On the Reels and Remix Controls page, choose whether you'd like everyone to have permission to remix your reels, people you follow only, or no one. (See Figure 13-15).**

6. **Make sure the Allow for Reels button is toggled to blue.**

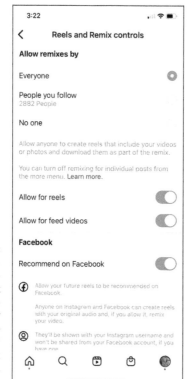

FIGURE 13-15: Choose who you'd like to grant permission to remix your reels on the Reels and remix controls page.

Making Use of Reels Insights

A newer feature that will surely be of interest to marketers and influencers is Reel Insights. You can now see how many views, likes, comments, shares, and saves happened on each reel. The insights also let you know how many accounts were reached by that reel. (See Figure 13-16.)

You can access Reels Insights by tapping on one of your Reels from your Reels profile tab, tapping the three dots on the lower right side of the screen, and then tapping Insights.

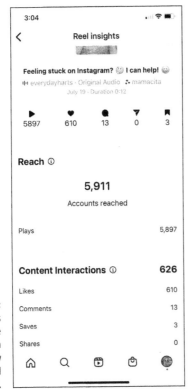

FIGURE 13-16: Reels Insights provide information about how your reel performed.

The Part of Tens

Know the top ten mistakes to avoid on Instagram.

Find inspiration from ten types of Instagram Reels and Stories.

Chapter **14**

Ten Things Not to Do on Instagram

I n this book, we provide lots of techniques to help you do well on Instagram. Sometimes, however, it helps to understand what *not* to do to ensure you create better content or build a better community with your followers.

If you want to make sure you make the best of Instagram, it can help to know what doesn't work or what annoys other people so you can avoid those mistakes. With the advice in this chapter, you'll avoid looking like a beginner!

Using the Same Name as Your Username

Nothing says "amateur" on Instagram faster than when your name and username are exactly the same.

The username (your @ name) is designed to be all lowercase and a string of words, names, or numbers perhaps separated by a period (.) or an underscore (_). The name of the account, however, should be in sentence format, utilizing capital letters, spacing, and even emojis.

If you want your username and your name to both be your *actual name,* your username might be @jenniferaniston while your name would be "Jennifer Aniston."

TIP

You can include emojis in your name to add more personality to it. Because some of the searchable criteria on Instagram are your name and username, if you want to be potentially found for something in particular (like your career), you may want that keyword to be part of your name. So, while you may keep your username as @jenniferaniston, your name might read "Jennifer Aniston, Actor." Just note that you're limited to 30 characters for your name, so your name can't be, "Jennifer Aniston, Best Known as Rachel from Friends." That kind of info is what your bio is for.

Turn to Chapter 2 if you need a refresher on how to set your username and name on Instagram.

Picking an Irrelevant Username

Your username is how you're recognized on Instagram. From posting to liking other content and more, you are your username. Therefore, it should appropriately reflect who you are.

WARNING

A random series of letters and numbers makes you hard to recognize. It also makes you look untrustworthy, and more people will be skeptical that your account is spam or fake, making them less likely to interact with you. An awkward or random username can also make it hard for people to find you if they're trying to spell your username to find you in search.

You can avoid these issues by picking a username that's easy to recognize and share! If your simple username is taken, you can try adding a period or underscore in between two words to make it slightly different than the other user's name.

The exception to this rule applies if you want to keep your account more private and *not* have it easily found in search. In this case, you may actually want to consider a username that is irrelevant to your actual name.

Using a Bad Profile Photo

One of the downsides to Instagram profile photos is that they get reduced to a very small size in the feed. Even a great full-size photo can look bad or poorly formatted when shrunk down to a circle one-half inch in diameter. In some cases, a perfectly normal photo looks inappropriate or resembles a completely different object when the size is dramatically reduced. Images with a lot of text also tend to look bad on Instagram — the text becomes illegible.

TIP

Choose an image that has good resolution, a clear object of focus, and a simple background. Avoid using a really busy image for your profile photo. If there are lots of people in the photo, or if it has a messy background, the context of the image will get lost when it's shrunk down.

Not Including a Bio

The description in your bio is an easy place to tell new people on Instagram who you are. Leaving this field blank is the equivalent of walking up to someone at a party, telling them your name, and then saying nothing else about yourself.

Your bio can say anything you want about who you are, what you do, what you're known for, and so on. Take the time to write something that helps you to connect with new people who find you on Instagram.

Ignoring Instagram Stories

More than 500 million people currently use Instagram stories every single day. With such a large audience and opportunity to connect with new people, you don't want to ignore this part of the app.

Instagram has put a big focus on story-formatted content, and it's expected that this type of content will only continue to grow in its creation and consumption. Ignoring stories means that you won't attract as many followers. Plus, if your existing followers prefer to consume story content and you're not creating that type of content, you'll miss out on the opportunities to connect with those followers.

The tips we give you in Chapters 7 and 8 help you create content to reach more people and keep your followers engaged with your stories.

Not Using Captions

Instagram is a visual platform, designed around photos and videos in the feed, Stories, and Reels. It wasn't designed for lots of text or long blocks to read through. And although a picture may speak a thousand words, a good Instagram caption can actually drive interactions with your followers.

REMEMBER

A photo or video on Instagram without a caption often lacks context. The caption is the opportunity to further convey your message or purpose of the post and connect with your followers. It's a place where you can ask questions, offer a call to action, or simply provide a story and background to the post. These types of interactions are critical to building relationships and driving conversations on Instagram. Don't leave a blank, empty caption on your posts!

Hashjacking

Hashjacking is the act of using trending hashtags on your posts to show up in front of new people. If you're attending New York Fashion Week and use the #nyfw hashtag in your posts, that's okay, because your content is actually related to the #nyfw hashtag. But if your post has nothing to do with New York Fashion Week, then using the #nyfw hashtag is hashjacking because you're using a popular hashtag just to try to get your image or video in front of a popular audience.

Hashjacking is heavily frowned upon. The content that shows up in trending tags but is completely irrelevant is usually ignored at best. If you're hoping to find new people, chances are, these people aren't going to follow you — plus, now they have a bad impression of you, so using this method can actually *hurt* your reputation. You may even find your content getting reported for spam by people who don't think your content belongs. And getting flagged for spam content will punish your account for at least 24 hours because you won't show up in other hashtag searches.

With the consequences of hashjacking, it's not worth using these hashtags unless, as we said, you actually have content related to the topic.

Tagging People Who Are Not in the Photo

You can easily tag other accounts in your Instagram posts. Tagging people is so easy, in fact, that people often take advantage of it! You should only tag people or brands that actually appear in the post itself.

For example, if you share a photo of you and your friends at a local restaurant, you could tag each of the people in the photo. You could also tag the restaurant's Instagram account because you're eating there. And you could even tag the brands for the clothing you're wearing in the photo. All of that would be acceptable because those accounts are in the photo you uploaded.

What you *don't* want to do is tag a bunch of other accounts of famous people, influencers you want to connect with, brands that aren't in the photo, or people you follow. Some people do this to try to grab the attention of these other accounts, but the attention they get is negative at best.

Another common tactic some people use is to post a motivational quote or similar content and then tag a bunch of people they want to "inspire." Unless these people are your friends, most people don't want to be tagged in your photos.

WARNING

These tagging tactics can often be viewed as spam and may get your account flagged for bad behavior. If you're regularly tagging people inappropriately, they may also unfollow you or block you. So, avoid these tactics and only tag the people or accounts who actually appear in the post.

Following Everyone Who Follows You

Instagram is a heavily engaged platform, and you'll see a lot of reciprocity where people follow you back if you follow them. But there is no expectation of reciprocal following. You don't need to follow everyone who follows you.

TIP

Instagram is meant to be fun. But it will only *be* fun if the content you see in your feed is content that you want to see. If it's full of your friends, family, favorite celebrities, brands you love, and accounts that inspire you, then you'll enjoy it, which means you'll log in more often, interact with more content, and enjoy the whole experience.

In contrast, if you follow hundreds of people you don't know simply because they followed you, your feed will include those people's posts, with their families, musings, random content, and whatever else they choose to post. Chances are that this content won't be relevant to you and you won't want to see it or interact it with it.

There's no need to fill your feed with things that don't matter to you! If someone follows you and you like their content, follow them back. But don't feel any obligation to follow everyone who follows you.

Using Automated Tools to Follow or Like Others

As you get deeper into the Instagram experience, you'll likely discover a variety of tools that offer services to augment your Instagram experience. Many of these apps or websites are legitimate tools that properly integrate with Instagram and can help you get more value out of Instagram.

Tools that offer to automate the process of liking posts, leaving comments, or following people for you are *not* these approved tools. In fact, any tool that does this is violating the Instagram application programming interface (API) and violating the terms of use you agreed to when you signed up for Instagram. Using any of these tools can put your account at risk of various penalties, up to and including your account being shut down. So don't rely on any tool that automates the interactions on Instagram for you!

You can, however, use a tool or app that helps you manage your Instagram account. Tools like Hootsuite (hootsuite.com) allow you to connect your Instagram account so that you can post to it from a desktop and manage your comments and other notifications. All of these dashboard tools, like Agorapulse (www.agorapulse.com), Sprout Social (sproutsocial.com), and Tailwind (www.tailwindapp.com), only integrate with Instagram Business profiles though. Again, this is due to the way the Instagram API is set up. If you're using a personal profile on Instagram, tools won't be able to integrate with your account.

Chapter **15**

Ten Types of Great Instagram Reels and Stories

There are so many things you can do with Instagram reels and stories! But what works best on Instagram? What types of reels and stories typically get more engagement?

In this chapter, we give you ten examples of content that generally performs better on Instagram. Two of the examples talk about trending audio, which we discuss in detail in Chapter 13.

Reels: Dancing

Before you roll your eyes, yes, dancing reels are very popular, especially among the younger crowd. Using trending audio and popular dance moves can bring a lot of views to your account if you do it regularly or put a special twist on a move. If dancing is for you, feel free to hop on the trend. If not, stay tuned because we have several other reels examples that don't involve dancing at all! (See Figure 15-1 for an example of a dancing reel.)

FIGURE 15-1: Instagram users @the. ford_sisters show off their latest moves using trending songs.

Reels: Educating

Instagram Reels have become an excellent platform for educating an audience about virtually anything! Are you a crafter? Show how to make a craft for a good friend. A science teacher? Explain how to easily remember the periodic table of elements. There are many ways to turn a short video into an educational tool. (See Figure 15-2.)

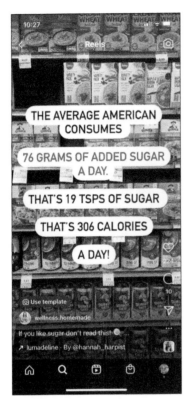

Reels: Lip Syncing

Another highly popular type of reel uses trending audio (usually someone talking rather than a song). The person filming the reel lip syncs to the audio and then relates the audio to their specific situation. People often get very creative using these lip syncs to sell products or services or just to make a funny statement about something other people can relate to. (See Figure 15-3.)

Reels: Green Screen Background

You've probably seen this in your feed, and may have wondered how it's done! Using a green screen filter within Instagram, users can upload a static image or video, then film themselves in front of it. The green screen filter can be found by tapping on the Effects button (before recording) and searching for "green screen."

Instagram users typically discuss what is in the image or video behind them. It can be an interesting way to talk about current events or a trending topic (see Figure 15-4).

FIGURE 15-4:
This image from @ gavinwakeupcall uses a green screen effect so he can discuss the new Hocus Pocus cereal.

Reels: Food & Travel

Food and travel reels are all over Instagram! They're the perfect way to share your vacation or the swanky new restaurant in town. Some foodies also showcase the food they ate that day by uploading multiple photos into a reel and setting it to music. Restaurants like Casa Ramos Restaurant (see Figure 15-5) share reels of their chef cooking orders in the kitchen to entice people to come try the food.

FIGURE 15-5:
In this reel
from @
casaramos-
restaurant,
the
restaurant
shares their
chef creating
one of their
signature
dishes.

Reels: Transitions

Transitions in a reel can help grab viewers' attention. A transition might be a change of clothes, throwing the video over to another person, or suddenly appearing somewhere else. There are many filters within Instagram you can use to create transitions (as discussed in Chapter 13), or you can create them through carefully editing multiple video uploads together (see Figure 15-6).

FIGURE 15-6: @purpledoguk uses a zoom-in feature on a camera to transition to the next part of her reel.

Stories: A Day in the Life

Stories are an excellent way to let your followers know more about you. One way is to share videos of what you did on a given day. You can share something exciting like an event or special occasion, or you may simply show what you did on an average Tuesday.

Chelsea Pietz shares multiple stories a day about her work, her chihuahuas, and her family, which lets her followers become familiar with her on a more intimate level (see Figure 15-7).

FIGURE 15-7:
@chelseapi-
etz shares
her daily life
through
video
stories.

Stories: Before and After

Before-and-after photos are always crowd pleasers. Who does-n't love a good makeover? In Figure 15-8, Christoph Trappe uses a story to show a before (left) and after (right) look at his office set-up. Stories are a good way to show the progress of a project over time.

FIGURE 15-8:
These two
stories
from
@christoph-
trappe show
the before
(left) and
after (right)
of his office
equipment.

Stories: Add Yours

The Add Yours sticker, a newer feature of Instagram Stories, lets users create a story and ask people to add their version of that story. In this one, author Nellie K. Neves shares a story of the last photo she took and asks others to add theirs. She is then able to see the posts that were added from that sticker. It's a fun way to engage with other people (see Figure 15-9).

FIGURE 15-9: @nellieknevesauthor used an Add Yours sticker on her story to get other people to add their story about the last photo they had taken.

Stories: Question Sticker

A question sticker is a fun way to get more engagement from your friends and followers (see Figure 15-10). You can add the sticker and ask any question you'd like. You'll get a notification when someone answers a question. By clicking on the notification, you can see what they said, and you can re-post those answers if you like.

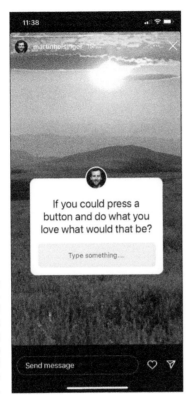

FIGURE 15-10:
@martinhols-
inger added
a Question
sticker to ask
his followers
what they'd
like to be
doing.

Index

game plan for Instagram Live, 188–189

group messages, 103–104

highlight galleries, 177–179

transitions for reels, 211–212

Creator account, 21

customizing highlights, 179

D

dancing reels, 231–232

A day in the life stories, 237–238

deleting

direct messages, 112–113

stickers, 158–159

stories from highlights, 181–182

video clips, 208

describing photos, 49

desktop web browsers, uploading videos via, 74

details, adding to videos, 68–69

dimensions, for stories, 174

Direct icon, 108

direct messages (DMs)

about, 88, 91–92

creating new group messages, 103–104

deleting unwanted messages, 112–113

navigating inbox, 108–111

Quick Sharing content via, 107–108

replying to, 104

sending in response to stories, 123

sharing

GIFs, 99–101

photos/videos via, 95–99

via, 167

starting new, 92–95

unsending, 94

using Live Chat in, 105–107

using voice messages, 101–102

discarding changes to photos, 47

DMs (direct messages)

about, 88, 91–92

creating new group messages, 103–104

deleting unwanted messages, 112–113

navigating inbox, 108–111

Quick Sharing content via, 107–108

replying to, 104

sending in response to stories, 123

sharing

GIFs, 99–101

photos/videos via, 95–99

via, 167

starting new, 92–95

unsending, 94

using Live Chat in, 105–107

using voice messages, 101–102

doodles, in stories, 160–162

drawing tools, accessing, 160

E

Edit screen, 48, 57–58

editing

captions, 49

photos, 44–47, 56, 58–59

stories, 172

educating reels, 232–233

Emoji stickers, 150

H

Hands-Free setting, 139
hashjacking, 227
hashtags
  in bios, 16
  finding people with, 88–89
  mistakes with, 227
heart icon, 122
highlight galleries, creating,
    177–179
Highlight icon, 179, 181
highlights
  about, 175–177
  adding
    from active stories, 177–178
    content to, 179–182
    from profiles, 177
  creating new highlight galleries,
    177–179
  customizing, 179
  deleting stories from, 181–182
  finding archived stories, 180–181
  fun ideas for, 182–183
  naming, 179
  sharing current stories, 179–180
Highlights tool, 46
Hootsuite, 229

I

icons
  A**, 162
  Camera, 40
  Direct, 108
  explained, 2–3
  Flash, 41, 63
  gear, 140
  heart, 122
  Highlight, 179, 181
  paper airplane, 171
  photo, 131
  plus (+), 40, 58, 62
  Recents, 41
  share, 171
  smiley face, 145
  Switch Camera, 40, 62
improving
  photos, 42–48
  videos, 65–70
inbox, navigating, 108–111
information, adding to photos, 59
Instagram algorithm, 28–30
Instagram Direct, 91
Instagram Live
  about, 185
  developing a game plan, 188–189
  getting started, 185–188
  inviting guests to broadcasts,
    189–190
  scheduling broadcasts, 190–191
Instagram Reels
  about, 195, 201
  adding text, 209–210
  as an algorithm factor, 28
  collaboration, 215–216
  creating transitions, 211–212
  dancing, 231–232
  deleting clips, 208
  educating, 232–233
  finding
    about, 195–198
    trending audio for, 206–207
  food & travel, 235–236
  green screen background,
    234–235
  lip syncing, 233–234

O

orientation, of video clips, 74

P

paper airplane icon, 171
pausing stories, 122
pen tools, 160, 161
people. *See also* following
  adding to video chars, 107
  tagging, 49–50, 227–228
personality, showcasing your, 126–128
photo icon, 131
Photo screen, 40, 42
Photo stickers, 157–158
photos
  about, 39
  adding
    about, 57–58
    information, 59
    location, 50–51
    to stories, 128–132
  applying filters, 44, 57–58
  before-and-after, 128
  candid, 126
  captions for, 226
  describing, 49
  editing, 44–47, 56, 58–59
  enriching, 48–52
  Facebook and, 51
  improving, 42–48
  options for, 49–52
  posting, 52–53
  for profiles, 225
  saving changes, 47–48
  selecting multiple, 55–57
  sharing
    about, 59
    via direct messages, 95–99
  tagging people, 49–50, 227–228
  taking, 40–42
  Tumblr and, 52
  turning commenting on/off, 52
  Twitter and, 51–52
  uploading
    from Camera Roll, 53–54
    multiple to one post, 55–59
    to stories, 131–132
Places feature, 83
planning stories, 125
Planoly, 125
Play button, 64
plus (+) icon, 40, 58, 62
Poll stickers, 152–153
posts/posting
  changing stories into regular, 173–174
  photos, 52–53
  sharing to stories, 170–173
  uploading multiple photos to one, 55–59
  videos, 69–70
privacy settings, modifying for accounts, 22–23
private accounts, 80
profile photos, choosing, 13–14
profiles
  about, 7
  adding
    highlights from, 177
    web addresses to bios, 18–19
  business upgrade for, 19–21

S

Saturation tool, 46

saving

  changes to photos, 47–48

  doodles, 162

  stories, 139–142

scheduling live broadcasts, 190–191

screen shots, of other people's stories, 166

scrolling feeds, 26–28

Search feature, 32–33, 82–84

searching

  about, 32–33

  direct messages, 111

  for recipients of direct messages, 98

selecting

  multiple photos, 55–57

  names, 9, 11–13

  photos for profiles, 225

  profile photos, 13–14

  usernames, 9–11, 223–335

sending

  direct messages (DMs)

    in response to Stories, 123

    without notifications, 95

  voice messages, 101–102

setup, of profiles, 7–23

Shadows tool, 46

Share button, 167

share icon, 171

sharing

  to Close Friends list, 167–170

  current stories, 179–180

  GIFs, 99–101

  Instagram posts and reels to stories, 170–173

  other people's stories, 165–166

  photos

    about, 59

    via direct message, 95–99

  Quick Sharing content, 107–108

  stories

    about, 125–128, 165–174

    to select people, 167–170

    via direct messages, 167

  videos

    from Camera Roll, 134

    via direct message, 95–99

Sharpen tool, 46

shutter button, 41, 63

sizing tool, 160

Slider stickers, 149–150

smiley face icon, 145

sound, toggling for video, 64

Sprout Social, 229

starting direct messages (DMs), 92–95

stickers

  about, 143–144

  Add Yours, 148

  Avatars, 151

  Captions, 154–156

  for causes, 158

  Chat, 153–154

  Countdown, 156–157

  deleting, 158–159

  Emoji, 150

  GIF, 148–149

  Link, 154

  Location, 144–146

  Mention, 146–147

  Music, 156–157

  Photo, 157–158

  Poll, 152–153

About the Authors

Jenn Herman is a social media consultant and globally recognized Instagram expert under the brand Jenn's Trends LLC. She is a sought-after speaker who provides tips, resources, and training for organizations of all sizes that need to structure their social media strategies.

Jenn has been featured in *Inc.*, *HuffPost*, *The Verge*, CBS Radio L.A., Fox News, Yahoo! Finance, and numerous other podcasts and publications. She is the author of *Ultimate Guide to Social Media Marketing* (Entrepreneur Press) as well as *Instagram For Business For Dummies*, 2nd Edition (Wiley). Jenn's Instagram username is @jenns_trends.

Corey Walker is the owner of The Marketing Specialist in El Dorado Hills, California. The Marketing Specialist offers social media strategy, content, ad management, and analytics, with a concentrated passion for Instagram and Facebook. She has managed the social media accounts of hospitals, medical groups, restaurants, real estate agents, online businesses, and publications. She is also coauthor of *Instagram For Business For Dummies* (Wiley). Corey's Instagram username is @coreycwalker.

Eric Butow is the owner of Butow Communications Group (BCG) in Jackson, California. BCG offers website design, online marketing, and technical documentation services for businesses. He has written 42 computing and user experience books. His most recent books include *Ultimate Guide to Social Media Marketing* (Entrepreneur Press), *Instagram For Business For Dummies*, 2nd Edition (Wiley), *MCA Microsoft Office Specialist Complete Study Guide* (Sybex), and *Digital Etiquette For Dummies* (Wiley).

When he's not working in (and on) his business or writing books, you can find Eric enjoying time with his friends, walking around the historic Gold Rush town of Jackson, and helping his mother manage her infant and toddler daycare business. Eric's Instagram username is @ericbutow.

Dedications

To my daughter, who continues to push me forward every day.
—Jenn Herman

To my husband, Les, and daughters, Kendall and Cameryn.
—Corey Walker

To all the daycare kids, who keep inspiring me.
—Eric Butow

Authors' Acknowledgments

We would like to thank the team of people who made this book happen. Our agent, Carole Jelen, was a huge help in getting this book off the ground. The team at Wiley, especially executive editor Steve Hayes, made this book possible. Rebecca Bollwitt offered lots of useful suggestions as our technical editor. Our families and friends supported us through all our late-night writing sessions. And a final thanks to you, for buying this book and being a part of the Instagram community we love!

Publisher's Acknowledgments

Acquisitions Editor: Kelsey Baird

Project Editor: Charlotte Kughen

Copy Editor: Christine Pingleton

Technical Editor: Rebecca Bollwitt

Sr. Editorial Assistant: Cherie Case

Production Editor: Saikarthick Kumarasamy

Cover Image: © pixelfit/Getty Images

Take dummies with you everywhere you go!

Whether you are excited about e-books, want more from the web, must have your mobile apps, or are swept up in social media, dummies makes everything easier.

Find us online!

dummies.com

Leverage the power

Dummies is the global leader in the reference category and one of the most trusted and highly regarded brands in the world. No longer just focused on books, customers now have access to the dummies content they need in the format they want. Together we'll craft a solution that engages your customers, stands out from the competition, and helps you meet your goals.

Advertising & Sponsorships

Connect with an engaged audience on a powerful multimedia site, and position your message alongside expert how-to content. Dummies.com is a one-stop shop for free, online information and know-how curated by a team of experts.

- Targeted ads
- Video
- Email Marketing

- Microsites
- Sweepstakes sponsorship

20 **MILLION** PAGE VIEWS EVERY SINGLE MONTH

15 MILLION **UNIQUE** VISITORS PER MONTH

43% OF ALL VISITORS ACCESS THE SITE VIA THEIR MOBILE DEVICES

700,000 NEWSLETTER SUBSCRIPTIONS TO THE INBOXES OF

300,000 UNIQUE INDIVIDUALS EVERY WEEK

# of dummies

Custom Publishing

Reach a global audience in any language by creating a solution that will differentiate you from competitors, amplify your message, and encourage customers to make a buying decision.

- Apps
- Books
- eBooks
- Video
- Audio
- Webinars

Brand Licensing & Content

Leverage the strength of the world's most popular reference brand to reach new audiences and channels of distribution.

For more information, visit **dummies.com/biz**

PERSONAL ENRICHMENT

9781119187790	9781119179030	9781119293354	9781119293347	9781119310068	9781119235606
USA $26.00	USA $21.99	USA $24.99	USA $22.99	USA $22.99	USA $24.99
CAN $31.99	CAN $25.99	CAN $29.99	CAN $27.99	CAN $27.99	CAN $29.99
UK £19.99	UK £16.99	UK £17.99	UK £16.99	UK £16.99	UK £17.99

9781119251163	9781119235491	9781119279952	9781119283133	9781119287117	9781119130246
USA $24.99	USA $26.99	USA $24.99	USA $24.99	USA $24.99	USA $22.99
CAN $29.99	CAN $31.99	CAN $29.99	CAN $29.99	CAN $29.99	CAN $27.99
UK £17.99	UK £19.99	UK £17.99	UK £17.99	UK £16.99	UK £16.99

PROFESSIONAL DEVELOPMENT

9781119311041	9781119255796	9781119293439	9781119281467	9781119280651	9781119251132	9781119310563
USA $24.99	USA $39.99	USA $26.99	USA $26.99	USA $29.99	USA $24.99	USA $34.00
CAN $29.99	CAN $47.99	CAN $31.99	CAN $31.99	CAN $35.99	CAN $29.99	CAN $41.99
UK £17.99	UK £27.99	UK £19.99	UK £19.99	UK £21.99	UK £17.99	UK £24.99

9781119181705	9781119263593	9781119257769	9781119293477	9781119265313	9781119239314	9781119293323
USA $29.99	USA $26.99	USA $29.99	USA $26.99	USA $24.99	USA $29.99	USA $29.99
CAN $35.99	CAN $31.99	CAN $35.99	CAN $31.99	CAN $29.99	CAN $35.99	CAN $35.99
UK £21.99	UK £19.99	UK £21.99	UK £19.99	UK £17.99	UK £21.99	UK £21.99

dummies.com

dummies
A Wiley Brand